T0286150

UNFORGIVABLE?

UNFORGIVABLE?

Exploring the Limits of Forgiveness

STEPHEN CHERRY

BLOOMSBURY CONTINUUM
LONDON • OXFORD • NEW YORK • NEW DELHI • SYDNEY

BLOOMSBURY CONTINUUM
Bloomsbury Publishing Plc
50 Bedford Square, London, WC1B 3DP, UK
29 Earlsfort Terrace, Dublin 2, Ireland

BLOOMSBURY, BLOOMSBURY CONTINUUM and the Diana logo are trademarks of Bloomsbury Publishing Plc

First published in Great Britain 2024

For legal purposes the Acknowledgements on p. 213 constitute an extension of this copyright page

A catalogue record for this book is available from the British Library

Library of Congress Cataloguing-in-Publication data has been applied for

ISBN: HB: 978-1-3994-0132-6; eBook: 978-1-3994-0131-9;
ePDF: 978-1-3994-0130-2

2 4 6 8 10 9 7 5 3 1

Typeset by Deanta Global Publishing Services, Chennai, India
Printed and bound in Great Britain by CPI Group (UK) Ltd,
Croydon CR0 4YY

For the harmed

Jesus said, 'It would be better for you if a millstone were hung around your neck and you were thrown into the sea than for you to cause one of these little ones to stumble.'

CONTENTS

CONTENT WARNING

This book is about forgiving and forgivability in the aftermath of serious, traumatic and life-changing harm. From the outset it necessarily discusses some of the most disturbing and distressing of experiences, including sexual assault, rape, torture, murder and genocide, and at times uses vocabulary which some may find offensive.

INTRODUCTION

As a young nun, Dianna Ortiz engaged in missionary and educational work in the north-west of Guatemala. In 1989, she was abducted at gunpoint from a convent retreat centre by security forces, blindfolded and taken directly to a secret prison. She was then subjected to degrading torture involving extreme physical, mental and sexual abuse. After 24 hours an American who was in attendance abruptly called a halt to the proceedings. He drove her away saying that he would take her to the nearby American embassy. She escaped from his car, but not before he had told her it was a case of mistaken identity and advised her to forgive her captors and torturers and forget about it.[1]

The role and agenda of this American remains a matter of some obscurity. Was he directing operations at this hell on earth? It is not clear. And whether he was or not, why did he suggest that she forgive? He knew he was talking to a nun, and might have supposed that to be a nun was to practise forgiveness come what may. Did he feel he was reminding her of her calling? Or was it more self-interested? Did he feel that if she forgave, then his own guilt and shame might be assuaged? Or was it a weird moment of consideration for *her*, the suggestion of forgiveness based on his belief that the trauma of the suffering would be easier to recover from if she were able to release her feelings of anger, hostility and resentment? Or did he see not only the look of brokenness and trauma in her eyes, but also the awakening of a cold vengefulness, a spirit he feared might lead her to vengeful action? We cannot know. What we do know is that this shadowy figure is not alone in recommending that the harmed forgive those who have harmed them.

But imagine if, rather than jumping from the car, Sister Ortiz had looked the man in the eye and said, 'And what do you think forgiveness might mean in this situation? What would it involve? Why would it be appropriate?'[2]

The variety of circumstances in which forgiveness might be sought, offered or recommended is huge, and ranges from trivial but upsetting matters at home, at work or in the local community to atrocities that have led to suffering on an unimaginable scale. Forgiveness may be relevant wherever human beings have been wrongly harmed. And it may be relevant both to those who have suffered – and to those who are responsible. In the twenty-first century the human family is wrestling with its conscience over the colonial and imperial ventures of recent centuries; north Atlantic countries are trying to understand afresh the moral horror of the slave trade and its repercussions in terms of race relations. We are acutely aware that the previous century was marred by two world wars, the second of which concluded only after two atomic bombs were detonated. The most extensive and ruthless attempt at genocide was perpetrated in parallel with the Second World War and, despite the impassioned cry of 'Never again', genocides have since been attempted elsewhere, notably in Rwanda and the Balkans.

Since the turn of the millennium we have seen the growth of terrorist activity, whether organized and strategic or perpetrated by maverick individuals, and the increased incidence of fatal shootings in the US and knife crimes in the UK. And suffering inflicted on the young and vulnerable by those who preyed on them for sexual gratification or abused them in other ways has been exposed not as an occasional breach of trust by a singularly corrupted individual, but as something endemic in the culture of power relations that was supported and sustained by institutions, which then sought to cover it up or minimize its reality and impact. Then there are serial killers. As I was completing this book the British paediatric nurse Lucy Letby was found guilty of murdering seven babies and attempting to kill six others. She will spend the rest of her life behind bars, as will Rosemary West who, with her husband Fred, was responsible for the abduction, torture and murder of at least nine young women and the murder of her stepdaughter, burying their remains in the yard of their home in Gloucester.

As a summary of the inflicted suffering of recent decades these brief paragraphs are indicative rather than comprehensive. Nonetheless, they represent something of the range of challenges it is right to present to anyone who would propose to consider forgiveness. All talk of forgiveness is in a sense addressed to those who are living in the aftermath of harm. This includes victims, survivors, perpetrators, those who are clear about what they have done and those who deny responsibility. Then there are witnesses or bystanders, each with their own sense of connection and empathy with those who inflicted the harm and those who suffered it.[3]

Forgiveness always addresses vulnerability and complexity; if the notion is introduced it is always into a situation where interpretations might be contested, and while books inevitably deal with words, much of what might be important after harm might not fit at all easily into words, sentences, paragraphs or chapters. There are different levels of emotional response, there may be pain and discomfort too deep for words – and forgiveness may happen without anything being said.

One of the classic moments of forgiveness in nineteenth-century English literature is when Charlotte Brontë's Jane Eyre forgives Mr Rochester shortly after he has been exposed as already married while she has been waiting at the altar to become his bride. His little speech of regret and remorse to her begins full of self-pity, but eventually he asks for forgiveness.

'Jane, I never meant to wound you thus. If the man who had but one little ewe lamb that was dear to him as a daughter, that ate of his bread and drank of his cup, and lay in his bosom, had by some mistake slaughtered it at the shambles, he would not have rued his bloody blunder more than I now rue mine. Will you ever forgive me?'[4]

Jane then speaks, but not to Rochester.

'Reader, I forgave him at the moment and on the spot. There was such deep remorse in his eye, such true pity in his tone, such manly energy in his manner; and besides, there was such unchanged love in his whole look and mien – I forgave him all: yet not in words, not outwardly; only at my heart's core.'

We might wonder if Mr Rochester would know he was forgiven – if he detected something in her demeanour – and whether the unspoken forgiveness was, in fact, forgiveness. Silence is famously hard to interpret. Clearly this was forgiveness that fell short of reconciliation, but equally it was clearly something. There are many responses someone might make in such circumstances that would clearly not be forgiveness, but if Jane calls it 'forgiveness' who is the reader to argue? Indeed, the reader is being directly addressed and informed. 'I forgave, but I said and revealed nothing.' Under the circumstances it is a subtle and deft relational move. Minimal forgiveness, or safe forgiveness, one might say, but real and meaningful nonetheless – at least to Jane and her audience.

Jane, of course, has received no advice ahead of this moment of silent forgiveness. Nor is she a natural-born forgiver. Earlier in the novel she comes across the notion and resists it strongly. But that is a different situation.

And that's important. Circumstances in which people might consider forgiveness to be relevant vary hugely. And yet attempts to theorize or talk in a general way about forgiveness invariably have to play down the differences between situations. This is a serious problem when it comes to the giving of advice or counsel on forgiveness, offering exemplars of heroic forgiveness or otherwise expounding its benefits – all of which are increasingly common. I want to suggest that a responsible approach to forgiveness involves tempering theories and abstract propositions not with caveats but with attention to actual and imagined circumstances, and recognition that what might be a good response in one situation might be dubious, unwise or even irresponsible in another. For instance, had Mr Rochester succeeded in bigamously marrying Jane, soon become physically and emotionally abusive and then one day, after she had recovered from a violent attack, come out with much the same speech of regret and remorse as we have just read, we would feel very differently about her turning to us and confiding, 'Reader, I forgave him.' We would want to answer her and say, 'No, that's not the right thing at all, Jane. You need to get out of that place.'

Forgiveness may have the potential to make a positively transformative difference after harm, but it also has the potential to make matters worse. This is why advice-giving needs to be subtle, humble and contextual. It is also why all talk and writing about forgiveness needs to be careful and non-prescriptive – especially when coming from a context in which forgiveness is a highly regarded virtue or has an odour of sanctity. It is vital that those convinced that forgiveness has great positive potential, whether as something that keeps relationships intact or, at a political level, as the catalyst of a new era of peace and prosperity after the horrors of the past, stopping the escalating cycles of violence in a retaliatory conflict by surprising, generous and public forgiving, are cautious and nuanced in their promotion of forgiveness.

Forgiveness can be wonderful, astonishing, transformative, but the stakes are very high when forgiveness is discussed, and so it is important for its proponents, whether of a religious or a secular perspective, to get beyond the clichés and into the deep and difficult issues that are never far from the surface. This will involve paying close and detailed attention to the impact of harm on the harmed, and also standing back and surveying the scene as though from a distance, or through the lens of personal imagination. We also need to consider carefully the extent to which our stories of damage and repair are embedded within a cultural architecture of beliefs, principles and hopes, and the noise in our minds created by exemplary stories, whether of the power of forgiveness or the satisfactions of revenge.

This book is an attempt to enter, as calmly but realistically as possible, a raging whirlpool: the conflicted, contested and frankly often extremely confusing debate, now several decades old, about forgiveness. The task is not to put forgiveness under the microscope and analyse it, which would only be adding to the growing library of books addressing the philosophy and ethics of forgiveness. Nor is this a book which outlines how to go about forgiving someone when it is difficult to do so. There are plenty of books that do that, and several therapeutic tools devised to facilitate forgiveness. Nor do I see it as my task to promote or praise forgiveness.

In fact, I have serious reservations about all of these ventures. For me the philosophy is often too dry and abstract and distant from experience – especially the experience of the harmed. The psychological and therapeutic material sometimes feels pushy and prescriptive. And the promotional material on forgiveness, if I may put it that way, whether religious or secular, can be naïve both in what it says and, more importantly, what it implies and suggests to those for whom forgiveness feels impossible or might actually be inappropriate.

This book, rather, tries to give a humane and humanistic account of forgiveness *and its limits*, paying particular attention to the reality and the needs of the harmed, while not neglecting the wider needs of society, or the interests and concerns of bystanders and onlookers with various degrees of connection to victims and survivors. Nor does it neglect the offenders, the violators and the perpetrators of injustice, wrongdoing and harm. Most importantly, it represents an effort not to perpetuate various mistakes in the way Christianity has often approached and promoted forgiveness.

I

BACKGROUND

I

Abuse

Let me introduce you to Chris Green. Chris is not a real person, but he came into my mind when I was thinking about the shortcomings of my previous book about forgiveness, *Healing Agony*.[1] I imagined him as someone who had experienced not one but two seriously wounding harms, who was influenced by, but not fully signed up to, Christianity and who had – and this is the moment where credibility is more seriously stretched – come across my earlier book. What, I asked myself, might such a person as Chris feel and think as they were reading it? And what might they write if it occurred to them to reach out to the author?

So I wrote a letter from Chris Green to myself. It was a challenging exercise, and a very helpful one. As I imagined what had happened to Chris and the impact of any sort of pro-forgiveness writing on him, I felt myself drawn more and more deeply into a troubling set of thoughts and emotional responses. Chris may be made up, but he gives voice to concerns and considerations that are very real, and which need serious and sustained attention.

Dear Stephen Cherry

I meant to write to you a long time ago about your book 'Healing Agony'. A friend passed me a copy about a year after my mother had been murdered. I was reluctant to read it at first, because I had become fed up with – well, quite sick of, actually – people giving me advice about forgiving the murderer and 'letting go of my anger' towards him. But because I remembered you from when you conducted my grandfather's funeral in Manchester, I thought I'd try a few pages.

I find it hard to say quite why, but for some reason your book did help me. I got the feeling that you weren't judging my lack of forgiveness, and that allowed me to accept just how bitter I had become, and that in turn seemed to unlock something inside me. I don't believe that I've forgiven the murderer, but something good happened as a result of reading your book, so I am very grateful that you wrote it.

But I still wonder whether I should take a further step and actually forgive the murderer. Though I do wonder what that would involve in practice, and what it would mean. He's in prison, and I don't feel that his sentence should be reduced, and I am not inclined to spend my time visiting him. I could write a letter, I suppose, but that doesn't seem to make sense either. 'Dear convict, it's OK, I have forgiven you. Enjoy the rest of your stay! All the best, your victim's son,' doesn't have the right feel to it at all.

But Stephen, there is another side to this letter. I've read your book twice now and have become quite cross about its shortcomings. You see, the murder of my mother isn't the only trauma I've had to endure in my life. I don't want to go into details, but I feel I must share with you that I am a survivor of childhood sexual abuse. In fact, the person who abused me was a clergyman, like you, and that's another reason I didn't want to read your book.

As a result of the abuse I experienced, I've been through every circle of hell. I won't say that my life was destroyed, but the experience scarred me deeply. I call myself a survivor and not a victim, but I can't say that I have got over it and I am not sure that I ever will. Stephen, why didn't you write about the trauma of sexual abuse in your book? Didn't you think the subject was important enough? Or was it just too difficult? Is the truth of the matter that such abuse is unforgivable – and you were afraid of saying so?

And I've got another question. It's a big one, perhaps a bigger one for you as a priest than for me as a part-time believer in God, part-time agnostic and part-time angry atheist. It's this. As I read your book, I found myself thinking, 'This man really thinks that Christianity has all the answers when it comes to forgiveness.' Do you really think that? I'd be very interested to know because, to be completely candid, I don't. Christianity talks a lot about forgiveness, but I'm really interested to know this: do you believe that Christianity has got forgiveness right?

Sorry to put my questions so bluntly, but this is how I feel. I'm still glad I read your book; it really helped me. But my questions just won't go away.

With thanks and best wishes

Chris Green

The sexual abuse of children and others who are vulnerable, perpetrated by people in positions of care and trust, has precipitated an extraordinary range of challenges for every organization or institution where it has happened, but especially the churches. I am not going to survey the whole sorry story here, but part of the motivation of this book is that I've come to the view that in church circles, and possibly more generally, naïve and distorted understandings of forgiveness have had a role in allowing the crisis to develop in the first place, and also got in the way of effective and healthy responses.

I am not alone in this. The British government's Independent Inquiry into Child Sexual Abuse, which focused on the Church of England and the Church in Wales, included in its 2022 report this comment:

> Forgiveness of those who have sinned is a core element of Anglican doctrine. Many members of the Church regard forgiveness as the appropriate response to any admission of wrongdoing. Some religious leaders use 'forgiveness' to justify a failure to respond appropriately to allegations. Timothy Storey, for example, was permitted to continue working with children after expressing 'remorse for everything he had done wrong'.[2]

The theology professor Linda Woodhead was quicker to grasp the need to take stock of Christian teaching regarding forgiveness, as part of the culture change in the Church deemed necessary if abuse were to be stopped. In an article in the *Church Times* in 2018 she argued that 'a theological audit is going to have to be part of the solution. An urgent place to start,' she continued,

> is a Christian understanding of forgiveness. In [the Diocese of] Chichester, a faulty doctrine of forgiveness was used by abusers to salve their consciences, by church officials to move on without dealing with the problem, and by parishioners and clergy to marginalize 'unchristian' victims and whistleblowers.[3]

Woodhead had undoubtedly put her finger on something extremely important, and so what I want to know is, is there a 'faulty doctrine of forgiveness'? If so, what's wrong with it, what harm does it cause, and can we find better ways to think and talk about forgiveness?

Others have been less measured in making a similar point. Dr Josephine Anne Stein, herself a survivor of ecclesiastical abuse, sees the abuse crisis as a profound pastoral failure. In a chapter in the book *Letters to a Broken Church* she argues that what is said, thought and done with regard to forgiveness and reconciliation is integral to what she believes might resolve the crisis: a 'highly professional Christian ministry'.

> Facile or convoluted theological approaches need to be challenged, such as misplaced pressure on survivors to rid themselves of the burden of abuse by putting it down and forgiving those who have [re-]abused them.
>
> Reconciliation is only possible if those responsible for ecclesiastical abuse confess what they have done, express true remorse and explain how they aim to set things right. Only then can they be reasonably be forgiven by survivors – and by God.[4]

One of the people I was able to speak to about her journey with forgiveness was Susan Waters. When Susan was seven and her brother Robert was aged ten, they were sexually abused by a swimming coach, Bob C., a predator to many other children. After a year, Susan stopped their outings together but Robert continued to abuse Susan in their home until she was 13 years old, was highly controlling and managed to pit the siblings against one another. I especially wanted to speak to Susan because of what I understood to be the religious aspects of her experience. We will turn to that, but it needs to be set in the wider context of the whole abusive story.

When Susan was young her parents were already relatively elderly. They had neither the understanding nor the resources to talk to their children about matters such as sexual abuse, and so there was much silence and hiding. This continued even after her brother had been accompanied by her father to the police station in 1970 to give evidence when Bob C. was at last arrested for his abuse of boys. He was never held to account for his abuse of girls.

Susan told me that Robert had initially been quite vulnerable. He was a 'sweet boy' and 'sensitive' and, as a consequence, a likely target for an abuser. In later life Robert presented himself as a fun uncle, but she allowed him only supervised access to her children, which she describes as her 'clear boundary'. One day, and without any warning, though Susan was in the room, Robert invited her children to go with him to Disneyland. Naturally they were very disappointed when their mother forbade the holiday. At the time, Susan told me, she felt doubly punished, the ongoing strain of keeping up the family façade compounded with terror that explaining to her parents the reason for her decision would see them react badly and even become unwell. But one day the edifice finally cracked. Robert's teasing brought Susan's youngest son to tears and she angrily ended the relationship.

It was only when her mother protested to Susan that they finally had a conversation about abuse. Her mother excused anything Robert had done on the grounds that 'he was *got at* as a boy'. Perhaps to her mother's surprise, Susan replied, 'Yes, me too.' But then she couldn't stop herself adding, 'Sorry, sorry, I'm so sorry.' Susan's feelings of shame, fear and guilt at disclosing a long-held secret erupted, and precipitated a complete nervous breakdown.

Robert later estranged himself from the whole family and moved to America. With him on the other side of the Atlantic Susan felt she could safely acknowledge their blood tie privately and love him from a distance. He had a long struggle with alcoholism and in 2019 committed suicide at the age of 64. After his death, and learning the extent of his ordeal, Susan felt able to forgive her brother, and subsequently had a profound sense that her forgiveness had been received.

The situation with Bob C. is different. Susan says she considers him to be a thief, who stole from their family. He threw a bomb into a household that had no way of responding, there was so much fear. She remains 'angered and disgusted', she told me, that he was never given a custodial sentence for his crimes. He was simply cautioned and fined £50. And yet, when Susan searched genealogical records to piece together something of Bob C.'s life, she found an unexpected surge of compassion when she came upon his date of birth. There was no significance in the date itself, but it reminded her that he too had once been a young innocent. She still wonders what happened to the child he once was to turn him into the man she knew.

Let's turn now to the religious side of the story. Susan is one of the people who, having suffered abuse, found no solace in Church teaching for her ongoing struggle with forgiveness. Under the pressure of regular abuse from her brother she became very withdrawn, even 'shut down', and failed her eleven-plus examination. In her isolation she still had a sense of a loving God being with her, someone to talk to who would understand. The forgiveness clause in the Lord's Prayer, however, was a spiritual agony, making her feel even worse about herself. And it was a grim Sunday when the sermon was based on the verse in Matthew's gospel about being reconciled with your *brother* before leaving a gift at the altar. At the time Susan was trying to figure out a way to stop seeing her brother without their parents asking too many questions. She knew this was not the time for reconciliation, but was nevertheless uncomfortable with the idea of directly contradicting a scriptural mandate.

In the 1980s, when as a mother herself she reflected on the innocence and vulnerability of children, she tried to find Christian resources to help and sustain her. But in vain. 'For a while I quietly tried to find some answers in Christian literature but all these were perfect stories of reconciliation. What I was looking for was permission to end the relationship with my brother, and I could not find this wisdom in Church teachings.'[5] She explained, 'Although I never lost my faith in Jesus or felt abandoned by him, it was through the Buddhist practice of loving-kindness that I came across the idea that when you cannot forgive another person you may forgive yourself for not forgiving. I discovered that forgiveness is a process. It takes time, and cannot be predicted or forced.'

It was that gentle encouragement to self-kindness that for her unlocked the possibility of forgiveness.

The extent of abuse, and the manner in which it has been denied and covered up and its impacts minimalized, have given Christian believers and Church leaders serious food for thought, but there is a far wider significance. This is not only because there has been abuse outside religious contexts, but also because the cultural and normative reach of Christianity has been extensive, and the idea that it is virtuous, noble and admirable to forgive, and churlish, mean or worse not to forgive, is commonplace well beyond the bounds of the Church. Believers and non-believers, religious people and avowed secularists can all feel pressure to forgive, and anxiety when they don't.

Examining this pressure, and giving an account of where it comes from, will involve digging into the way in which the concept of forgiveness has been developed, practised and promoted, especially in recent decades. I will focus on the impact of Christian thinking and practice on forgiveness not only because I believe Woodhead and the IICSA are correct to suspect that a 'faulty doctrine of forgiveness' has had a role in the sexual abuse debacle in the Church and more widely, but also because in recent years Christian leaders have felt it appropriate not only to encourage the practice of forgiveness in their communities but also to speak more widely about it, promoting its superiority over alternative responses to having been wronged or harmed.

Many of the great Christian leaders of recent decades have had a strong message on forgiveness, which they have proclaimed from the public square as well as the pulpit. I am thinking of Martin Luther King, John Paul II and Desmond Tutu. The current Archbishop of Canterbury, Justin Welby, is also a strong proponent of forgiveness as something that has much to offer today's world, which he has described as 'very, very unforgiving'. As we shall see, there were some good local and contextual reasons for Dr King, Pope John Paul and Archbishop Tutu to promote forgiveness. And Archbishop Welby is deeply aware of the tendency of those who differ on matters like sexuality or doctrine to denigrate and deprecate one another. He also speaks from the new reality of 'culture wars', which sees hostility not only towards those who hold certain views but also towards those who merely misspeak in certain ways, thereby revealing, it is claimed, a deep-seated and unacceptable attitude, whether that be racist, sexist, ablest, ageist or transphobic.

It is admirable, right and impressive that these leaders are prepared to enter the forcefields of controversy, prejudice and anger with the message of forgiveness. And yet questions of the sort raised in my imagined letter from Chris Green, and by the child abuse crisis and its complex aftermath, are not to be dismissed. What do we think about forgiveness? Is it a meaningful notion, and if so, when is it appropriate? There must be situations in which it seems to be just 11 letters strung together, but does this reveal the actual meaninglessness of forgiveness, or does it somehow point to something superlatively important and ethically sublime?

Having imagined the letter from Chris, I found myself wanting to reply. But if giving voice to his experiences, his burdens and questions reflected changes in my own thinking and awareness, it had by no means made me able to offer a quick set of answers. Chris was quite right: in my previous book I had not engaged with the question of forgiveness after sexual abuse. And yes, it had been too difficult. Over a decade later it is still difficult, but that is no excuse for avoiding it. It would be a mistake, however, to consider whether there can be forgiveness in the aftermath of sexual abuse in isolation. There are other situations where there is a strong case for saying that we have reached, or perhaps gone well beyond, the limits of forgiveness. Are there, at the human level, unforgivable actions? Are there people who have become, perhaps for a combination of reasons, unforgivable?

It is the thought of the sexual abuse of children that has taken me to this admittedly chilling territory, but there are other experiences that force the question just as acutely. When you pause to think about it, the range of situations which raise a serious question mark over the very notion of forgiveness, or at least prompt a discussion about its limits, is huge. Deeply troubled by these challenges to what I once believed the orthodox understanding that where there had been harm there should be forgiveness, I have found it helpful to continue writing letters to myself, the author of my previous book.

2

Letters

Dear Stephen

I am writing to you because you have written about forgiveness. I'm an older man now and I've seen many bad things happen in this life. I've certainly been on the receiving end of bad treatment, and I guess I've hurt a few people along the way. I mean you can't please all the people all the time – especially in business.

But I wanted to write to you about something else. I've had three children. Two lads and a daughter, Kate. She's clever and savvy. Didn't go to Uni but wants to start a business so I give her a lot of pre-inheritance – and I mean 'a lot' – and a lot of advice. She does really well. And full credit to her. I'm looking over her shoulder, but it's her work. And does she work! All hours. She gets married to Simon and they seem a great couple. No kids but that's the way it is sometimes. Then she becomes tired and loses a bit of dexterity and then a bit of movement. They test for everything but it turns out its Motor Neurone Disease or ALS as my American friends call it. Slow moving but completely incurable. She loses more and more bodily control and has to sell the business. Makes a fortune. But has no energy. She's slowly dying and utterly dependent.

And that's when it happens. Simon starts to live a double life. Money starts pouring out of the account. He's got a secret new girlfriend and, while Kate's lying at home – has a live-in career now – he's off on holiday with her. Business trip to New York, he says. Ten days in Manhattan. I wasn't born yesterday.

And that's when Kate died. While he was away.

I haven't spoken to him since. He sold the house and bought a bigger one for him and madam. They like entertaining I'm told, and she has three kids who live there half the time.

One of my sons is a minister. He keeps saying, 'Dad, it's the story of the Prodigal Son. You'll feel so much better if you forgive Simon.'

I just shake my head. I don't want to feel better. He betrayed her. He's got the money. He's got life. Why should I pretend it's all alright really?

If I'm wrong not to forgive – well so be it. I'm in the wrong. But at least I'm true to myself – and true to Kate.

Sincerely

David

Dear Sir

I have never written to an author before but, well, here it goes. Healing agony – nice idea. And the book was OK. But it's left me hungry and thirsty. You see, I can cope when bad things happen. My husband was rough with me, so I hit him back. Then he apologized. I said, 'that's fine, but if you do it again, I'll hit you very hard where you don't want to be hit'. He said

'OK, deal'. Then I forgave him. Talk about healing agony. If he hits me again, he knows what's coming.

But forgiveness – it doesn't begin and end with a thump or a slap, or even with a bit of playing away from home if you know what I mean. People are people, and we can take these things in our stride. No, what I'm talking about isn't the sins of my loved ones, but the offences of those who hate me. It's racism. It's white superiority. It's Windrush and the Home Office. It's Stephen Lawrence. It's slavery. It's why we protest that black lives matter because people go on as if they don't. It's the prison population in the US. Why do you think it's full of black boys and men?

'All things are connected', said Chief Seattle. That's one true thing, but my question for you, book writer, is how you connect these sad, horrible, horrendous realities with forgiveness. Where's the healing agony in racial injustice? You tell me, because I can't see it, though I say my prayers with a faithful heart I'm no Jesus. I can't say father forgive the racists. I don't know what it means.

May God bless you, my white brother, but I tell you this, you can forgive people for what they do and for what they've done. You can forgive them if they hit you or hurt you or steal from you or tell you lies or betray you or think up some other way to let you down. But you can't forgive someone for hating you. There's no healing agony for that!

I don't think that racists are going to rot in hell. But I think the Lord's going to roast their toes a little bit if they don't repent of their disgusting attitudes and actions. And some of them, they've got so much repenting to do that those flames are going to lick up a long way higher than their toes unless they jump to it. Have you read anything about the slave trade? I mean, what actually happened then? The Middle Passage, the selling, the whipping, the endless work, the terrible food, the abuse of body, mind and spirit.

Should I go on? Forgiveness has to be a big word if it's an answer to all this. A very big word. The biggest! So maybe forgiveness is God. Or maybe God is forgiveness. I don't know how to talk like this; but if you ask me, I'd say God should be justice, God should be truth. And the truth is that there's a whole lot of stuff that's never going to find any forgiveness. Well, that's as I see it. There's no excuse for hatred. And no forgiving it either. You just have to stop it.

Your sister

Gloria

Dear Reverend

I'm guessing we are about the same age. But unlike you I grew up in Belfast and at the age of 13 was throwing stones at British soldiers. By the time I was 20 I'd shot a few Protestants and set a few bombs. I spent the best years of my life in prison. Now I'm free. Thank God for Good Friday!

But I'm not really free. I'm in a prison in my heart. I'm captive to my years of stone-throwing, shooting, bombing and bullying others to do the same. No, I'm not free.

You talk about forgiveness! I can't tell you the number of times I've been to confession. We did that in the Troubles and the priest said what we'd done was OK. They had to, but what's worse is they believed it. But I've stopped now because it doesn't work. No confession for me any more. They can mind their own business. In prison I'd go along. I'd hear myself saying all those things again and again, but I'd walk away with the same heavy feet and the same hunched shoulders.

I suppose God does forgive. It's his business. Didn't someone say that? But what about the wee kids of the young men I killed? And their wives? And their mothers too – don't believe I don't think about that. I've thought of everything. Of everyone who was hurt by my actions – by me. Lives ruined. Lives ended. What do you think I dream about? Protestant funerals! Funerals that I've had a hand in making. I don't suppose those heartbroken people would ever forgive me. And I don't think they <u>should</u> forgive me. If they told me they did I'd tell them to get lost. Damn it, I don't forgive myself. How could I? It's done. Nothing can put it right. Nothing. All those words. Those church words. Your words, Father. Should I call you Father? I never know with Protestants. Anyway, priest words are useless words, Reverend.

There's another thing too. I know you've got a picture of me in your head as a gunman, balaclava and all. A Provo. Fair enough, but I look respectable now. Maybe driving taxis isn't a big deal, but it's a better job than it used to be back in those dark days. But that's not the point. The point is, how does a 13-year-old boy get to be throwing stones at soldiers?

Sure, I threw the stones, but the stone-throwing wasn't down to me. I was just teenage cannon fodder. If I was African, you'd call me a child soldier. Yes, I'm guilty as hell. Guilty of hell. Just think of bomb blasts. But before that I was innocent, and when I was innocent, I was used. I don't mean abused. Not in that sense, but I was definitely exploited. My innocence was exploited. It was destroyed. The child in me was eliminated. It'll never come back. I wish it would.

Just a teenager, I was throwing stones, a little cog in, what shall we call it – a terrorist machine, a people's army? I was just a pawn in someone else's game of chess. What does a 13-year-old know about history or religion or politics? Slogans. That's all. Slogans and hate. And that's all you need to make a mess of a country; all you need to end lives and ruin communities.

And that all got started because of stupid, stupid, stupid political mistakes by people who never even touched a stone, never made a petrol bomb, never picked up a gun, never heard the sounds or smelt the smells of a bloody bomb blast.

You want people to forgive each other. I'm too sad to forgive myself but far too fxxxxxxing angry to forgive the people who set the Troubles off in the first place.

Sorry this is a long letter, but the world's a nasty place, Reverend, and forgiveness doesn't even touch the sides. But don't get me wrong, I'm not angry with you. I'm sure you mean well. But we can't undo the past. Can't rub it out. Black spots on my soul. No washing day for them.

Respectfully

Michael

Dear Steve!

I'm writing you from Rwanda. My pastor gave me your book about forgiveness. It's not bad, but it's not for me. You say that we forgive others when we reach out to them with empathy. Yes, and you call it distasteful empathy because we hate ourselves even as we feel it because we know how disgusting their actions have been.

Let me tell you, there are plenty of people I find abhorrent, but the last thing I want to do . . . actually, the one thing I will definitely never do, is to reach out to them with empathy.

You might remember that shortly after our terrible genocide came to an end the great Bishop Desmond Tutu came to preach forgiveness and reconciliation. I can tell you he got no standing ovation from me! After he'd finished, we sat down quietly with him and we said, 'Bishop, let us take you to church . . .' Of course, he said 'yes'. But let me tell you about that church.

You might be thinking – nice retreat in the rainforest with maybe a family of gorillas high up in the trees round about. No, my friend, this church is the least sacred, most damnable place in my whole desecrated country. It was a real church, for sure. A place where hundreds of people rushed to sanctuary. Indeed, they were sent there for sanctuary by the very people who planned their slaughter. Men, women, children and babies too – of course the little ones. Slashed and cut to death. Left to bleed and die. And women and children raped in front of their loved ones before the machete took away the last remnants of any human life from those wretched bodies and tormented souls. That is the church where we took the bishop of reconciliation and forgiveness.

'Now, Bishop', we said, 'how can we make peace with this situation?' Reconcile? Forgive? Our mind's eye cannot hold the memories of this suffering. Our hearts cannot bear the grief. So, what are our hands to do? Reach out in a gesture of friendship?

I mean, Lord have mercy!

'Bishop', we said, 'forgiveness is not a word to use here. It would be poison on our lips.'

Yours

Ingabere

To reiterate, these letters are all from imagined correspondents who read my earlier book on forgiveness in situations where people have been seriously and irrevocably harmed, and where 'forgiveness' might have been suggested. They have not always interpreted the book accurately or fairly. What I wrote back in 2012 was by no means straightforwardly enthusiastic about forgiveness. In fact, one of the reasons why I thought of the form of imaginary letters pushing back against the message of forgiveness was that I received letters that were appreciative of the book's relatively accommodating view of non-forgiveness. And while I had not broached child abuse directly, there were readers who made the connections – for instance, a woman who knows I am using her correspondence here but wishes to remain anonymous. I will call her Jennifer.

My good friend N. introduced me to your writings when he sent me a copy of a sermon of yours which I very much enjoyed. As a result I looked you up and found the *Healing Agony*. So, a few weeks on, I am writing to say thank you for this book.

I had a difficult time as a child, with an abusive father and an acquiescent mother. It was a tough childhood. As a Christian, albeit a new recruit, I have found it hard to forgive my parents, but this left me with a sense of guilt, a sense that somehow I couldn't really be a Christian if I couldn't forgive. I would go to —, near where I live, and sometimes light a candle for my parents and ask God to look after them and forgive them. It was the best I could do. Your book has given me permission to 'hold my grudges provisionally, lightly letting them go when they have done their work'. I realized they had indeed done their work and I no longer needed to hold on to them. But, having said that, I still bear some small grudge, but I can live comfortably with this.

What I like about your book is its understanding and honesty. Forgiveness is complicated. I have found most of what I have read in theological books and texts advocates forgiveness. 'If God can, so can/must we,' is what I hear. My parents died some years ago, and I have wanted to forgive them for many a year, for my sake, perhaps, more than for theirs! I think that unless you have been through some trauma imposed upon you by another, it is difficult for others to understand the nature of forgiveness, either through a Christian's eyes or through those of a person without faith.

I could continue, as there was so much in your book that resonated with me and helped me to understand from a Christian point of view. N. has taught me much (vast amounts, in fact!), but the one thing I have learnt more recently from him is that there are many

> different ways to interpret Christ's teachings. Your book sees forgiveness in all its complexity and degrees. The words of yours which make me well up at every reading are, 'True forgiveness, like true prayer, is aspiration, struggle and openness to the will and love of God.'

I remain grateful to Jennifer for reaching out with this feedback. It has been consoling as the shortcomings of my efforts have loomed in my mind. I am glad that my advice to hold grudges lightly (rather than banish them quickly or let them rule the psychological roost) resonated helpfully, and still feel it is helpful to describe true forgiveness as 'aspiration, struggle and openness'. However, I realize now that, while that was a step in the right direction, it didn't go far enough into this deeply difficult and troublesome territory. The letters from imaginary correspondents haunt my mind and demand, not *answers* exactly, but a deeper response.

I could have outlined the points made in the letters in a more objective, analytical and dry manner, of course, but I opted for letters to convey some of the complexity and intensity of the feeling that an experience is beyond forgiveness, and to engage the reader's empathy. Empathy in forgiveness is hugely important, but difficult to articulate clearly, partly because empathy itself is complex and contested. One of the ideas in my earlier book I have come to reflect on most seriously is my suggestion that for forgiveness to develop, a 'distasteful empathy' of the survivor for the perpetrator is necessary. The implication is that the survivor needs to overcome that distaste in order to get some sense of the humanity of the harmer.

While I still think this can be appropriate, in situations where the harm is inflicted for an extended period by someone with psychological power over another empathy should be set aside because of the danger of it being manipulated. This is one of my concerns about approaches to forgiveness developed in one context being applied in another without sufficient thought, and why I wrote a critique of empathy into the letter from Ingabere in Rwanda, though it could also have featured in the letter from Gloria, had her focus been on domestic abuse and infidelity and not on what she saw as the worse issue of racism and hatred. And Chris Green might have expressed a concern too. It is one thing for someone who has been hurt and angered by the actions of their peers to engage in distasteful empathy, quite another for someone trapped in an abusive relationship after an extended period of grooming in which they had no idea what was going on.

Any thought of distasteful empathy in the context of ongoing abuse or exploitation now seems to me evidently ill-advised and out of place. And yet it also seems problematic to be advocating *against* empathy; just as it feels awkward to be urging caution and circumspection when it comes to forgiveness. That there are limits to the possibilities of empathy across the divide of prejudicial and cruel hatred is, when you step back and prioritize your compassion and empathy not for perpetrators but for victims and survivors, all too evident. What matters is not losing all sense of the humanity of the perpetrator. What I failed to say in *Healing Agony* is that there are routes to this that do not depend on the potentially dangerous and dubious practice of empathy.

These letters flag a number of important issues. Chris Green's revealed that, while he has made some progress on forgiving his mother's murderer, he seemed quite stuck when it came to the priest who abused him as a child. This raises questions about the difference between the possibilities of forgiveness for the same person in different situations. That from David, whose daughter Kate died of motor neurone disease (or ALS, as it's known in the States), was angrily dismissive of the possibility of naïve forgiveness, rejecting the relevance of the story of the Prodigal Son and his minister son's argument that forgiving would make him feel better. The letter from the former terrorist in Northern Ireland ran many themes together, from the impossibility of self-forgiveness to his insistence that remaining unforgiven was the only ethical and decent course, while at the same time railing against the politicians who had created the situation in which he was himself used and exploited. And then there was the letter from Rwanda, putting the case that arguments and approaches effective when South Africa made its transition to democracy were not relevant or appropriate in a situation of attempted genocide.

We are exploring forgiveness from the perspective of its limits. The question is not only when, whether and why it might be good to promote it, but also in which circumstances forgiveness becomes inadvisable, inappropriate or even wrong. Before delving into that I want to get a sense of how the current interest in and understanding of forgiveness has developed.

3

Promise

In her Christmas Day message in 1987, Queen Elizabeth II reflected on the dangers of intolerance escalating into violence, and the importance of mutual respect and understanding. At the heart of her thoughts was the IRA's bombing of a Remembrance Day service that year in the town of Enniskillen. The Queen drew particular attention to 'Mr Gordon Wilson', commenting that he had 'impressed the whole world by the depth of his forgiveness'.

On 11 November 1987, Gordon Wilson, draper, and Methodist local preacher, had been attending the outdoor Remembrance Day service in Enniskillen with his daughter Marie. The IRA set and detonated a bomb that caused huge destruction, terrible injuries and 12 deaths. Marie was terribly injured by the blast and died in her father's arms. Later that day he spoke to the BBC. His words were transmitted to the nation. The following morning he gave a long interview to the *Today* programme on BBC Radio 4. Many people were surprised and moved by the deliberate and calm honesty of his response, and in particular these words about the bombers. 'I bear no ill-will,' he said. 'I bear no grudge.' Historians will debate whether such moments are of real political significance. But it was early in 1988, the year after Enniskillen, that Gerry Adams of Sinn Fein and John Hume of the SDLP first met. Mr Wilson may have been anticipating a change in attitudes, or he may have precipitated it, or perhaps both. It was certainly around this time that the word 'forgiveness' became significantly more prominent.

Mr Wilson did not use the word himself; he never said that he forgave the bombers. In many subsequent interviews he made it clear that he felt he had no right to do any such thing. Reflecting on his intervention almost four decades later, we might note that there was no high-flown language, no talk of the need for forgiveness or reconciliation, or even for peace or justice. He spoke from the heart and touched people's hearts by saying that he bore 'no ill-will' and 'no grudge'. Never have negatives been heard so positively. While some may have called for revenge or retaliation, Mr Wilson's attitude made such words seem ugly, inappropriate and demeaning. Indeed, he himself called them 'dirty'. But he found the right, healing and inspiring words at the right time. Ever since he has been understood and presented as a man of forgiveness.

The desire for peace in Northern Ireland had certainly been articulated before then, most clearly in the declaration of the 'People for Peace' of 1976. That declaration did not use the language of forgiveness. But when Mr Wilson spoke, although he carefully avoided the word 'forgiveness', forgiveness was heard. It was a new dawn for the notion of forgiveness, and journalists quickly got into the habit of asking victims of violence whether they forgave. In 1987, forgiveness's time had come in an unprecedented way. This is when its renaissance began.

On the night of 14 November 1940, almost half a century before the Enniskillen bombing, the ancient cathedral of Coventry was razed to the ground by bombers of the Luftwaffe. Four hundred and forty-nine German bombers were involved, and the bombing went on for 11 hours. Coventry was targeted because its factories were so important to the war effort. The strategy was to inflict debilitating damage on the whole city, though ironically the factories were not hugely damaged and back in production within days. The death toll was so great, however, with 550 people dead, that for the first time in Great Britain people were buried in mass graves. The Provost of the Cathedral, the Very Revd Richard (Dick) Howard, responded to all this not with angry vengefulness or hatred but with words of forgiveness. While the cathedral was still smouldering, he wrote the words 'Father, forgive' on the sanctuary wall. He also made a cross out of fallen rafters and, shortly afterwards, a further cross from nails that had fallen to the floor. When the new cathedral was built and adorned, that cross of nails was given a central place, and the words 'Father, forgive' are now permanently inscribed into the floor and west doors.

Coventry Cathedral has become an international icon for peacemaking and the pursuit of reconciliation between former enemies. 'Forgiveness' is etched into its very fabric. Despite the prominence and power of the Coventry witness, however, the notion of forgiveness didn't catch the public imagination in anything like the same way in the 1940s and 1950s as it did in the late 1980s and 1990s. As C. S. Lewis observed in his post-war radio talks in the United States that were to become the bestselling and hugely influential book, *Mere Christianity*,

> Everyone says forgiveness is a lovely idea, until they have something to forgive, as we had during the war. And then, to mention the subject at all is to be greeted with howls of anger. It is not that people think this too high and difficult a virtue: it is that they think it hateful and contemptible. That sort of talk makes them sick, they say. And half of you already want to ask me, 'I wonder how you'd feel about forgiving the Gestapo if you were a Pole or a Jew?'[1]

Lewis goes on to argue that forgiveness is intrinsic to Christianity. Provost Howard doubtless agreed, and at Coventry Cathedral resources were found for an influential ministry of reconciliation and to create the worldwide Community of the Cross of Nails. These were significant developments and had their origins in Howard's forgiving response, but they cannot be compared with the range and intensity of interest in forgiveness since the late 1980s.

Forgiveness caught the imagination of many in the late 1980s and the 1990s in a way that didn't happen in the 1940s, 1950s or 1960s. Major political transitions and highly publicized personal responses to terrible harm both played their part, but other factors included an increased interest in the psychological aspects of life, in particular mental health. This was reflected in the publication in 1984 of a small book about interpersonal forgiveness, written by a pastor in the United States, Lewis Smedes. The seminal role this book had was noted by Everett Worthington, the pioneer of the psychological study of forgiveness, in *Handbook of Forgiveness*. 'Scientific study of forgiveness began in earnest only in the mid-1980s,' he writes,

> and has accelerated since that time. It started in the therapeutic community after the publication of a trade book, *Forgive and Forget: Healing the Hurts We Don't Deserve*, by Lewis Smedes (1984). Ironically, Smedes was neither a clinician nor a scientist. He was a theologian. Yet he started a movement within therapy and science that revolved around the idea that forgiveness can benefit a person's mental health and well-being. That message resonated with therapists, who began to write about how to promote forgiveness in healing for problems in anger, lack of hope, depression and trauma. In addition, couples counselling and family therapy were natural laboratories for observing the harm of unforgiveness and the healing benefits of forgiveness.[2]

Smedes' approach was to present forgiveness as a God-given way to overcome the painful legacy of being harmed. 'Forgiveness is God's invention,' he wrote, 'for coming to terms with a world in which, despite their best intentions, people are unfair to each other and hurt each other deeply. He began by forgiving us. And he invites us to forgive each other.'[3] Smedes presents forgiveness as 'love's toughest work, and love's biggest risk', and as something that 'seems almost unnatural'. Smedes' book articulated what seemed like profound insights at the time – particularly that forgiveness was a process, and that it should be distinguished from forgetting, excusing, 'smothering conflict', accepting people and tolerance. These sentiments became standard fare in many publications that followed and, while there are many different versions of 'the forgiveness process', Smedes' simple 'We hurt, we hate, we heal ourselves and we come together' has many typical features.

It is clear that for him forgiveness is about working towards reconciliation, and the decisive thing is that, having been plunged into hatred, the harmed person shouldn't passively accept that as their final destination, nor should they escalate their negative feelings into bitterness or vengefulness or acts of retribution. Rather they should set about the project of their own healing. This is the point at which forgiveness takes place. It involves the faculty that Smedes describes as 'magic eyes', a change of perspective or what has sometimes been called a 'reframing' of the harming action. Rather than see the person who inflicted the harm through the lens of that harm and its impact, Smedes' advice was to try to see the person as you saw them before the harm, especially if that vision of them was of their vulnerability and neediness. The thought behind the idea is that hatred blinds us to a full and proper perception of the one who harmed us, but when we do manage to see them differently, we develop a different feeling towards them. And that is forgiveness. As he puts it, 'Forgiving, then, is a new vision and a new feeling that is given to the person who forgives.' That is not the end, or 'climax', as he puts it, of forgiveness. This comes in the embrace of two people simultaneously released from the grip of a painful past. However, while Smedes has a vision of reconciliation as the ultimate fulfilment of forgiveness, the key to it is finding a way to avoid or get beyond hatred.

Worthington describes Smedes as a theologian, and the book is an early and important example of mixing together a religious perspective with interpersonal forgiveness. The message is that although forgiveness is difficult, it is better to forgive than not to, and important to offer people assistance so that they can. There can be real merit in helping people to forgive when they experience difficulty in doing so, especially when there is a negative over-reaction to an offence or injury. But the project is, in my view, flawed by several false and unnecessary moves. Principal is the notion that human forgiveness can be modelled on God's forgiveness. Second is that the trajectory or *telos* of forgiveness is reconciliation. The third is that forgiveness here is seen as a process initiated by the harmed person, and largely a set of self-repairing inner changes.

The first two points here are intrinsic to most Christian thinking about forgiveness but, as Worthington indicates, the real energy was in the secular and psychological response to Smedes' suggestions. The idea that divine forgiveness was the model for, or even relevant to, human forgiveness was quickly dropped by the therapeutic and scientific communities, and a distance soon opened up between the notions of forgiveness and reconciliation. This in turn led to the development of what is reasonably called 'therapeutic forgiveness', a whole industry of research and newly developed interventions to help those debilitated not by the original harm they have experienced but by their own responses to that harm, to drop or moderate their anger, desire for vengeance, resentment or hatred. Therapeutic forgiveness was in its infancy when South Africa began its political transition from apartheid, and was given an extraordinary boost by the stories of forgiveness that emerged from that journey. In his post-apartheid career Desmond Tutu, who chaired the iconic South African Truth and Reconciliation Commission, became the inspiration and patron of many projects and centres which, as the new millennium dawned, were established to find ways forward other than retaliatory violence and hatred. We shall turn to the impact of Desmond Tutu in Chapter 6. But first I want to explore more deeply our contemporary fascination with forgiveness, and the extent to which it remains controversial.

4

FASCINATION

Stories in which a seriously harmed person comes to the point of forgiveness can be compelling and heartwarming. They draw us to the most difficult depths of human experience and show us that there can be a way forward, even if it doesn't appear quickly. They can inspire us with a sense of wonder that anyone could be courageous and generous enough to forgive after suffering so much; and humble us as we think we could never do the same. We are fascinated and touched by stories of forgiveness in deep and complex ways.

The level of interest in forgiveness can have never been higher than it is today. Novels, movies, soap operas and dramas often deal with forgiveness or forgiveness-related questions. More and more memoirs are written and published which explore the way in which the experience of harm has been overcome. Some actively promote forgiveness, while others take a more detached and discursive approach to how life has moved on.

One of the more famous examples, especially since it was adapted for the screen, is Eric Lomax's *The Railway Man*, in which he writes of how he came to forgive the interpreter who was present when he was waterboarded in a Japanese prisoner-of-war camp.[1] Much more recent, and one that puts forgiveness squarely to the fore, is Stephanie Cassatly's *Notice of Release*, in which she describes, as the book's subtitle has it, *A Daughter's Journey to Forgive her Mother's Killer*.[2] An example of parental forgiveness is Azim Khamisa's *From Murder to Forgiveness: A Father's Journey*.[3]

Camilla Carr and John James were humanitarian workers in Chechnya when they were kidnapped and incarcerated. Their experiences included mental torture and threat of execution, and Camilla was repeatedly raped. When they arrived home after their release in 1998 they were greeted by a gaggle of press and invited to speak. 'One thing we are keen to get across', explained Camilla, 'is that we feel no bitterness towards our captors, for we know their actions are a result of war trauma'.[4] Personal accounts of moving forward after rape are rarer than forgiveness memoirs after the murder of a loved one. A profound example is Susan Brison's *Aftermath*.[5] Brison doesn't use the language of forgiveness at all, but talks of healing and forgetting through a process of narration. In the course of her account she recalls comments made by religious family members, who unhelpfully assumed that she had already 'recovered' and moved on, and that she would have been strengthened and edified by the experience. The disinclination of the religious to engage with the pain of the harmed is, sadly, one of the subtle pressures that has driven our understanding of forgiveness in an unhelpful direction. And it makes me wonder how often our appreciation of forgiveness stories can be self-indulgent. 'Oh good, she has forgiven. That's all right, then.'

A memoir very much dedicated to forgiveness after rape is *South of Forgiveness*, co-written by Thordis Elva and Tom Stranger. As in many cases, the rape was perpetrated within the context of an existing relationship. Elva was 16 and Stranger 18. She was Icelandic and he was visiting from Australia. As Elva put it in a TED talk, 'I was in love for the first time. I felt like the luckiest girl in the world.'[6] At a Christmas party she got so drunk that medical support was called. Stranger, however, was the one who took her back to her room and placed her on her bed. Then he took off her clothes and raped her. She was unable to physically resist, but counted each of the 7,200 seconds during the two hours the attack persisted. Despite her suffering, both physical damage in the short term and then severe mental decline and turning to self-harm of various kinds, Elva did not recognize that what had happened was rape until it was too late to press charges. However, after eight years she wrote to Stranger and initiated not only an exchange of emails but also a visit to Cape Town in pursuit of forgiveness. The book describes in extraordinary and compelling detail how forgiveness emerged from a complex, uncertain, subtle and lengthy relational process; a process which, we might add, was untheorized and unguided. The night before the two of them leave South Africa an unspoken and implicit forgiveness that has slowly developed is finally articulated. 'Before I know it the words are on my tongue,' writes Elva.

> 'I realize I've never said "I forgive you" to your face, but I do. I forgive you, Tom.'
>
> His eyes open wide. 'Oh my God, did you just say that?' he gasps.

> Before I know it, his arms wrap around me and sweep me up tight against him like a rag doll. I hug him back, surprised by his strong reaction when the sobs tear through his throat. His crying shakes my body, and I hear myself whisper into his ear: 'It's over. I forgive you. It's over.'
>
> We embrace for a long while before he lets go of me, wipes a tear from his cheek, and says, 'I accept your forgiveness.'[7]

It undoubtedly is a forgiveness story. It is also a reconciliation story, and a story of deep healing and liberation – Stranger's – whose final words in the book are, 'If forgiveness was a religion, I'd be a follower. My soul feels free.'[8]

In March 2017 Elva and Stranger were due to appear at the Women of the World Festival at the South Bank Centre in London, but when the organizers received a petition of 2,000 signatures expressing concern about how the event would impact on other survivors the pair were dropped, though their talk was rescheduled a few days later at the same venue.

This was not the only controversy on their international book tour. Sometimes there were protests against Stranger's presence, with placards proclaiming, 'There's a rapist in the room' – a reminder, if one were needed, of how much is at stake in telling this story, and that personal decisions to forgive by the victim do not constrain the attitudes of others towards the perpetrator.

Questions abound. We might ask, which is the better attitude, Elva's forgiveness or that of the protesters? And was Elva's decision to forgive simply her private business, or something for which she is accountable to the wider community of victims and potential victims? These are perhaps matters for discussion rather than answer. But the fact that the story of the aftermath of rape is presented as a 'forgiveness story' rather than a 'calling to account story' is, I feel, significant. The position of those who see this as a story that might perpetuate a culture of impunity around sexual violence is understandable, especially since the implications of Elva not appreciating that what had happened was rape until it was too late to bring charges are not extensively explored.

Nevertheless, *South of Forgiveness* offers a complex and idiosyncratic narrative of forgiveness. It was not quick, unilateral or easy, and yet the thought of it, and the hope, particularly Elva's, that it might be possible to move on from a toxic combination of self-blame, the desire to hurt back, hatred and anger, is what propels the narrative. A period of almost 20 years passes between the rape and its forgiveness, and at every stage the process is driven by Elva, the survivor. And 'survivor' is the right, self-chosen, word, not for her post-forgiveness condition but as a token of her determination not to be defined as 'damaged, dishonoured, less-than'; a choice balanced by the decision to refer to Stranger not as 'the rapist' but 'the perpetrator', as 'rapist' implies words like 'monster' and 'unhuman', which would prevent any form of mutual moving forward. *South of Forgiveness* starts with rape and ends with a visit to the Rape Crisis Centre in Cape Town and the discovery that 'South Africa has some of the highest reported rape statistics in the world and a province that is home to a city that is dubbed the Capital of Rape.'[9] Elva reflects on her privilege in being able to attend to the damage inflicted on her and engage in a process of deep and extended healing, recognizing that for many who experience rape there is no choice but to accept and make the best of it.

Some might see a positive in introducing the concept of forgiveness to the aftermath of rape – it is manifestly different from denial, cover-up or acceptance. But does personal forgiveness encourage or weaken protest against unacceptable, harmful and traumatizing actions? Is forgiveness a force for personal healing and for social good? Or does it facilitate the former while undermining the latter? To many, Stranger would seem to have 'got away with it'. At one level this is undoubtedly true. But it was the statute of limitations that got him his amnesty, not Elva's drawing him into a process that would ultimately end in forgiveness.

Yes, the ultimate forgiveness scene takes place on a beach just after sunset in one of the most beautiful cities in the world – but it might have taken place in a prison visitor centre. Would that have been a better, more just, more socially impactful story? Would it ever have happened? And what is this ultimately all about?

Asked on BBC's *Newsnight* programme on 15 March 2017 whether they were now 'friends', Elva said they were not, but that they were 'collaborators on a project that extends well beyond us'. That is a project to raise awareness about sexual violence, and in particular to make the point that perpetrators are not monsters. *South of Forgiveness* is a remarkable but troubling testimony, offering many fascinating insights into the way forgiveness is understood today and how it might work out in practice, and throwing up many important social and ethical questions. It is a compelling story of forgiveness but an uncomfortable, awkward and unsettling one.

Far more numerous than published memoirs exploring forgiveness are the 'forgiveness stories' in the media. These are stories of people personally damaged or bereaved by violent or otherwise hurtful actions, who have found a way to forgive the person responsible. Some have a clearly religious angle and motivation, but most do not, and an increasing number reflect the therapeutic understanding that it is by letting go of negative feelings and excessive rumination that a survivor is able to stop the harm they experienced having further deleterious impacts on their life.

When it comes to the collection and curation of forgiveness stories there is nothing that stands comparison with the work of the Forgiveness Project in the UK. This represents a sustained engagement with the stories of people from all over the world who have struggled to avoid retaliation, vengefulness or hatred in the aftermath of harmful experiences. It began in 2004 as a small exhibition of photographs and stories at the Oxo Gallery on London's South Bank and has expanded to include a website which presents over 200 forgiveness stories. Other products of the project include podcasts and a series of programmes on BBC Radio 4, a small graphic book entitled *Forgiveness is Really Strange* and two full-length books by Marina Cantacuzino, who founded it. Cantacuzino is a journalist by training, and her work seeks to draw attention to non-retaliatory or violent responses to harm, and is driven on by a curiosity and human interest in the variety of ways in which people navigate their way forward.[10]

There is no one definition of forgiveness within the Forgiveness Project, but there is endless fascination in how people find their way to a future after harm, and the diverse alternatives to the pathway of hatred or retribution. Sometimes this involves a real struggle to overcome vindictive emotions or the desire to get even. On other occasions forgiveness seems to come more naturally to people. The storytelling is non-judgemental and open, typically eschewing the conventional plot of 'This awful thing happened to me but [drum roll] I reached out and forgave.' It's more like, 'This is what happened and, as time went by, it opened up for me a whole range of questions about who I am and what I could possibly do to move on without making matters worse. It's difficult to describe, but here is my story . . .' The Forgiveness Project absolutely avoids taking a preachy or proselytizing approach to forgiveness. The desire is to examine and probe what people think and feel after harm has been inflicted and to explore the various tactics they use to move on – without responding in ways that make matters worse.

There are those, of course, who don't take a cool, observational approach to forgiveness, but rather see it as positive and virtuous, and to be promoted to others and developed as a personal skill. For many months a small book that presented over 20 'inspiring stories from those who have overcome the unforgivable' was on the *New York Times* bestseller list. There is a huge appetite for such inspiration, but the book does not go down well with all audiences. I asked four Cambridge students to read it as part of a project that considered forgiveness stories alongside theories of forgiveness. It would be an understatement to say that they did not like it. They got very cross about it. One, who had already become something of an expert on the mega-church scene in the States, quickly identified it as from that stable. It wasn't overtly flagged up as a 'Christian lifestyle' book, but to the knowing eye that's exactly what it was. The book is Katherine Schwarzenegger Pratt's *The Gift of Forgiveness.* [11]

Katherine Schwarzenegger Pratt is described on the cover, under a smiley photograph, as 'bestselling author, animal advocate, daughter [of Arnold] sister, wife [of Chris] and stepmom'. When she was a child she fell out with a best friend who lied to her about a play date. As a result, the two were estranged for 20 years. When the former friends reconnected, Schwarzenegger Pratt decided that she needed to do some 'serious forgiveness work'. She sought guidance from clergy, went into therapy and spoke to everyone she could about it. This in turn led on to interviewing the 20-plus people whose stories she tells in her book. Here we meet people who have been kidnapped, raped, abused, tortured, exploited, bereaved by murder or terrorism, or otherwise had their lives torn apart, and yet have a story for her to tell about forgiveness. Each chapter ends with a short testimony from Schwarzenegger Pratt on what she has learnt and how she can apply it in her own life. At the end of the book there are lined pages on which the reader is invited to draft a letter to someone they want to forgive, or by whom they would like to be forgiven – maybe even themself. The cover illustration is a brown paper package tied up with string.

In the introduction, Schwarzenegger Pratt acknowledges that some readers might feel that 'having a fight with your best friend sounds trivial,' but assures them it is not. 'If I didn't get this right, I would have that pit in my stomach for the rest of my life. I knew it would end up traumatizing me.'[12]

My students felt that the appropriation of the stories of the grievously harmed in the interests of supporting the better practice of forgiveness by those who enjoy remarkably privileged lives was more than distasteful. However, the book remains useful simply for the wide range of situations it references in which forgiveness could be found, and for the tenacity, honesty and generosity of those who were able to forgive the unforgivable – and because it so evidently sets a very high bar for forgiveness, while not naïve about its difficulties. 'Forgiveness', Schwarzenegger Pratt tells us, 'isn't about simply saying, "I forgive you"– it's about doing the work of *letting go*, which for me has proven to be the gift that goes on giving.'[13]

Katherine Schwarzenegger Pratt is a positive enthusiast for forgiveness, and the nature and the popularity of her book tell us much about how forgiveness is regarded and approached today. It offers a way of moving on after harm has been inflicted that has no downside. It is virtuous on the part of the harmed, freeing for the harmer but, most significantly, comforting and edifying for the observer. But that isn't the whole story.

5

Controversy

When Marina Cantacuzino launched the Forgiveness Project many people assumed it was a Christian proselytizing venture, which created a suspicion she had to work hard to overcome. Consequently she often made a point of defining it as 'grittily secular'. Interestingly, the common assumption of those coming across the project now is not that it is Christian but rather that is some kind of 'New Age' venture – associating forgiveness with a broader and less organized system of alternative approaches to life's challenges and mysteries. I once asked Marina's successor as director of the project, Rachel Bird, if she felt its work might be made easier by dropping the very word 'forgiveness', with all its complex associations and connotations. 'The word itself can cut through a room like a guillotine,' she said, 'dividing it right down the middle', and yes, the pros and cons of the name have been periodically discussed. Nonetheless, it remains the *Forgiveness* Project, not 'the project to investigate and share in a non-evaluative way non-retaliatory, non-vengeful or hate-avoiding responses to having been harmed'.

'Forgiveness' can be a noisy, sometimes unhelpfully distracting and baggage-laden word, but there isn't a better one to point to the possibility of a response to harm which is not over-determined by the harm itself, but open to more promising and peaceful pathways to the future. That very broad description reflects how the territory of interpersonal forgiveness is widely understood and chronicled today. But it remains hard to imagine the word *not* being associated with controversy, widely divergent opinions and powerful feelings.

Forgiveness's capacity to spark controversy and polarize opinion is well illustrated by the theatre. Shelagh Stephenson's play *The Long Road* begins with 18-year-old Danny having been killed in a random stabbing in London. After the first phase of her desperate grief, his mother decides she wants to walk the path of forgiveness and puts a lot of time and energy into trying to relate to the imprisoned young woman who stabbed him. The father, on the other hand, is full of anger, which slowly pushes him towards despair and alcoholic oblivion. Meanwhile the younger sibling, devastated as he is by the loss of his brother, feels he has lost his place in the household to the ghost of his brother – both parents being so preoccupied with what has happened in the past while the day-to-day challenges of his adolescent life continues.[1]

In Peter Shaffer's *The Gift of the Gorgon* Edward and Helen Damson respond to the news of Gordon Wilson having forgiven the IRA bombers in Enniskillen in diametrically opposed ways. Edward responds, 'Incredible! What a terrible thing to say!' Helen takes the contrary view. 'I think it's glorious! It's possibly the most moving thing I've ever heard.'[2]

Nina Raine's 2017 play *Consent* explores the entangled personal relationships, loyalties, weaknesses and agendas behind the possibility of courtroom justice. Two friends, Edward and Jake, are the prosecuting and defending barristers in a rape case the petitioner, Gayle, seems doomed to lose – especially when her background of depression is used against her while the accused's history of sexual offences is not mentioned. The play ends with Edward begging his wife Kitty for forgiveness for marital rape.[3]

'What's wrong with vengeance?' Kitty asks earlier in the play, to be told that those who forgive unconditionally live longer. This, however, is not enough to make her a forgiver. 'I said, I'm sorry,' says Edward.

'What?' she replies. When he gets down on his knees she says, 'What are you *doing*?'

'I'm saying sorry,' he replies. 'Forgive me.'

'Oh get *up*.'

'Please.'

So it continues until she says, 'Stop it. Please.'

'Why?'

'Because.'

'Why?'

'Because you're making me feel sorry for you,' says a tearful Kitty – words which lead into the last words of the play: 'Forgive me. Fucking forgive me.'

The play sets huge questions for its audience. If justice is sometimes so unlikely, might forgiveness offer a better way forward? But what if the victim doesn't see the point, and longs for justice even if it is unattainable? And might not seeking forgiveness from someone who is reluctant to give it – especially if we seek it with a performance of sorrow and self-humiliation – only make the petitioner seem, and feel, ridiculous? In which case, who is in the wrong – the person disinclined to forgive, or the offender who hasn't worked out that something more than dramatic sorrow and self-pity are needed to unlock the possibility of forgiveness?

Forgiveness in real life can certainly be controversial, and much can be learnt from reflecting on that controversy itself – something Figen Murray discovered after she publicly forgave Salman Abedi, who killed 22 people at the Manchester Arena in May 2017 with a homemade suicide bomb as thousands were leaving an Ariana Grande concert. Figen's son, Martyn Hett, was one of the victims. Her forgiveness was not instantaneous but flowed naturally from her response to two images. The first was a photograph of Abedi himself, the second of five Muslims making a protective cordon around a man who had sought to attack worshippers, slipped and fallen and found himself in danger of being attacked by a mob.

I was able to talk to Figen just before writing this book. I knew of her remarkable lobbying for Martyn's Law – legislation to oblige entertainment venues to have due regard for security – and wanted to hear how she responded to the personal hostility, abuse and trolling that had been unleashed by her public forgiveness. What I had not expected was to hear her say that she found it easy to forgive; that it had come naturally to her in the early days of her grief. But the more we talked, the more I found the word 'easy' convincing.

What sealed it was the extent to which Figen had accepted the death of her son as a life-changing tragedy for her. She had given up her counselling and coaching work and dedicated herself to becoming educated and connected enough to be an effective advocate for security, and found ways to work for peace and the good of others at several levels. But what struck me most was that she was a woman with an extraordinary capacity for empathy.

In the introduction I stressed how there are times when empathy could be a problematic or even dangerous emotion for victims or survivors, but in this particular situation – the horror so stark, the losses so acute, the cultural barriers so high, and the perpetrator so young, indeed actually dead – the role of empathy in facilitating forgiveness seemed very positive as well as very significant. Figen told me that when she saw a photograph of Abedi in the newspaper her first thought was, 'Ah, oh my goodness, you are so young.' In her counselling, she went on, she always encouraged people not to react but to see the bigger picture. 'I also did that. I looked so far back that I saw the terrorist as a newborn baby. And I thought, "No, you were born innocent. Nobody's born that bad and that dark in your [*sic*] mind. Somebody poisoned your mind." And that helped also with the forgiveness thing'. Figen also told me that she had never had angry feelings or thought 'if only' or 'what if'; nor did she ever get depressed. Her only emotional response was that of sadness, a sadness which persisted six years on. This was not self-interested forgiving. It was forgiveness as part of a complex, multidimensional, socially responsible and hopeful response to aching tragedy.

As for the hostility of others and the trolling, the impact can't really be known from outside, but in so far as *my* empathy allows, my hunch is that the pain of bereavement would put the irritation of being hounded on social media somewhat in the shade.

And what of the bereaved who did not favour forgiveness? Where are they coming from? Some would be against it, feeling it in some way minimized either their loss or the egregiousness of the bomber's act, or his responsibility for it. Some might have wanted to clarify that she was not forgiving in their name (she never claimed to, of course). But there is also the nature and meaning of forgiveness. Might some of Figen's trolls have thought she was purporting to absolve the bomber; to speak in an authoritative way about how he would be presented before the throne of heaven? Or were they concerned that the one who killed their loved one might be remembered as 'the forgiven bomber'? Such concerns might not be fully conscious, but in play nonetheless, because we are often muddled when we think or talk about forgiveness. We vacillate between thinking of it as something that indelibly impacts on a perpetrator and as something that has nothing to do with them at all, and is solely about the injured person achieving peace of mind.

Figen's forgiveness, it seems to me, couldn't really be either of these. It resides somewhere in between – or perhaps might be better imagined as the third point of a triangle. This is forgiveness born not out of the desire for freedom from guilt or resentment, but out of hope. This forgiveness is not about absolving the other or eliminating bad feelings from the harmed psyche, or about proclaiming the beginnings of interpersonal reconciliation. It is about acknowledging and possibly even embracing the full sadness of a situation, with all the relevant emotions and life changes, while allowing a combination of human sympathy and hope to have a transformative say. It involves, as the old cliché goes, giving up all hope of a better past; but more important is the hope regarding the future. Not naïve optimism that forgiving will somehow be a cure for the agony of grief, but a genuine and active hope that attitudes as well as actions can make a difference to the way the future unfolds.

Different occasions of forgiveness spark different controversies. Possibly the most famous and discussed example in the United States is the forgiving of Dylann Roof, the young white supremacist who attended a Bible study class at Mother Emmanuel Church in Charleston in June 2015. During the closing prayer he drew out his pistol and started shooting the participants. Nine were killed outright, including the pastor, the Reverend Clementia Pinkney. Others were injured or traumatized. The impact on family members, the church and the wider community was devastating, and shockwaves were felt across the States. Two days after the shooting, Roof appeared in court and, as the names of the killed were read out, so the magistrate invited members of their family to speak. The third victim was 70-year-old Ethel Lance. When her name was called, her daughter Nadine Collier rose to speak. She turned to Roof and said,

> I just want everybody to know I forgive you! You took something very precious away from me . . . But I forgive you! And have mercy on your soul. You. Hurt. Me! You hurt a lot of people . . . But God forgives you. And I forgive you.[4]

Several others also spoke in terms of forgiving Roof, and word quickly travelled. President Obama, who was ultimately to speak at the funeral of the Reverend Pinkney, promptly decided that his message would emphasize the forgiving response rather than reiterate gun crime statistics.

Since then Charleston has been presented as a beacon of forgiveness in an unforgiving world. The reality, however, is not so straightforward. In the *New York Times* Roxanne Gay wrote that it was precisely because of the racist and historical context of the murder that she would *not* be offering forgiveness.

> I do not forgive Dylann Roof, a racist terrorist whose name I hate saying or knowing. I have no immediate connection to what happened in Charleston, SC, last week beyond my humanity and my blackness, but I do not foresee ever forgiving his crimes, and I am wholly at ease with that choice [. . .]
>
> My lack of forgiveness serves as a reminder that there are some acts that are so terrible that we should recognize them as such. We should recognize them as beyond forgiving [. . .]
>
> I am particularly unwilling to forgive those who show no remorse, who don't demonstrate any interest in reconciliation. I do not believe there has been enough time since this terrorist attack for anyone to forgive. [. . .]
>
> The call for forgiveness is a painfully familiar refrain when black people suffer. White people embrace narratives about forgiveness so they can pretend the world is a fairer place than it actually is, and that racism is merely a vestige of a painful past instead of this indelible part of our present.[5]

Gay's position is that there are situations in which it is wrong to forgive, and so even if emotionally she were inclined to be forgiving, she would restrain herself from doing so as a witness to the depth of what was wrong. She articulates the need for principled unforgiveness.

A similar but different form of principled unforgiveness was articulated by the Holocaust survivor Primo Levi, the Italian chemist whose writings have had a major impact on how the Holocaust has been understood and interpreted. Readers of his works have often remarked on the absence in his writing of hatred and the desire for revenge. Does this mean that Levi has forgiven? While he is congenitally not given to hatred or revenge, he explains, he could imagine being tempted to it if he came face to face with 'one of our persecutors of those days'. It is a temptation he would resist, just as he avoided writing his account of the Holocaust in emotional language. However, none of this, he asserts, should be mistaken for forgiveness. 'No, I have not forgiven any of the culprits, nor am I willing to forgive a single one of them.' Levi goes on to say that he *would* forgive if he came across such a person and discovered that he had become 'conscious of the crime and errors of Italian and foreign Fascism and is determined to condemn them, uproot them, from his conscience and for that of others'.[6]

Forgiveness can be admirable, beautiful, impressive, moving and wonderful, but although it is sometimes right, it is not always. That is why the subtitle of the book refers to the limits of forgiveness. What, if anything, can be said about the limits of the possibilities of forgiveness and, more importantly, what can be said about what lies beyond those limits? Is it necessarily the case that the only alternative to forgiveness is vengeance and hatred? Or might there be ways of withholding forgiveness that are calm, healthy, ethical, wise and even spiritual?

I believe there are, and this is a truth that has been all but hidden over the years during which forgiveness has had a remarkable renaissance. I also believe that we are often muddled by forgiveness, that forgiveness has a shadow side we ignore at our peril, and that Christian enthusiasm for forgiveness has led to it being over-promoted and overvalued to such an extent that the question of the limits of forgiveness has often been obscured if not lost. As I have said, it is hard to imagine forgiveness not being associated with controversy.

6

Tutu

In 1990 Nelson Mandela was freed from prison in South Africa, and in 1994 the new country had democratic elections and established a constitution which featured reconciliation as one of its seven pillars. This led to the creation of the South African Truth and Reconciliation Commission (TRC) presided over by Archbishop Desmond Tutu, which was to play a significant role in preventing the much anticipated 'bloodbath', as many put it, of vengeance. The first truth commission had taken place in Argentina and reported in 1983, while Chile had the first 'truth and reconciliation commission', which reported in 1990. It was the South Africa TRC, however, that projected forgiveness into the public mind in an unprecedented way, reflecting the reconciliatory temper and strategy of those who came to power in the new republic but also a peculiar mix of psychological, religious and political ideas, and indeed some linguistic confusions. In one set of hearings the TRC offered amnesty to people who were prepared to tell the truth about crimes they'd committed while serving or opposing the apartheid state, provided they could establish that their actions were politically motivated.

It cannot be denied that amnesty is part of the larger family of forgiveness-like concepts; it belongs in the forgiveness word-pond, but, as Jacques Derrida and others have pointed out, the differences are fundamental. 'Amnesty' is a decision by a relevant authority not to prosecute, and 'forgiveness' is a transformative response to those who are responsible for harm inflicted by wrongdoing. Those who sought amnesty did not need to profess anything about how they felt about what they confessed to. There was no requirement for apology or expression of remorse and therefore, crucially, no requirement on the commissioners to assess the validity or sincerity of any such statements. Nevertheless, in some of the talk around the TRC 'amnesty' and 'forgiveness' have been used interchangeably, and this has contributed to the exaggerated sense that the TRC was an agency of forgiveness, projecting it into the political arena.

In a parallel set of hearings, the stories of those who had suffered personally under apartheid were heard and reparations promised to those who established that their human rights had been 'grossly violated'. This was also an arena of acknowledgement and witness. But as the hearings developed, so something else emerged. There was witness not only to suffering, loss and trauma but also to how at least some of those adjudged to be victims felt towards those who had harmed them or killed their loved ones. It is here that instances of personal forgiveness emerged.

At the time Archbishop Tutu enthusiastically advocated for the amnesty approach and warmly encouraged the personal acts of forgiveness, continuing to do so in *No Future Without Forgiveness*, his account of the TRC and its merits, which came out just one year after the official report of the TRC was published.[1] One of the remarkable features of the book is the extent to which it put a Christian interpretation on a process integral to the transition *from* a Christian apartheid state to a democratic and secular republic. As Jacques Derrida put it, 'he christianised the language of an institution uniquely destined to treat "politically" motivated crimes'.[2] The Dutch scholar Jan Frans van Dijkhuizen makes a similar point: 'Desmond Tutu famously reads the hearings by the South African TRC in deeply religious terms, involving the full vocabulary of divine forgiveness, including contrition, confession and redemption.'[3]

'The affirmation of forgiveness is one of the TRC's most prominent legacies,' wrote the philosopher Diane Enns, 'and it would be hard to overestimate the impact it has had on the post-conflict reconstruction field.'[4] This grand statement is true but also understates things. The impact of the TRC in turning Desmond Tutu into an expert on and advocate for forgiveness had a far wider impact.

In *No Future Without Forgiveness*, Archbishop Tutu presents forgiveness as the lens through which to view the whole TRC process. Individual acts of forgiveness are praised, on the grounds that it was the readiness of people to forgive and, in a phrase he often repeated, 'let bygones be bygones' that shaped the relatively peaceful transition in South Africa. After the TRC, Tutu went on to be an international spokesman and consultant on forgiveness, supporting the development of numerous institutes, especially in North America, and encouraging what he would jokingly refer to as the 'forgiveness industry'. We might also note how the Archbishop was invited to take the TRC's insights to troubled parts of the world including Northern Ireland, Rwanda and the Middle East. His message of forgiveness was not received with universal appreciation, although in North America and Great Britain, and especially in Christian circles, the response was often extremely warm, even adulatory. Here was an archbishop who had taken a core Christian principle and shown it to be transformative in both personal and political life.

Tutu's thoughts about forgiveness grew and developed after apartheid. In 2014, together with his daughter Mpho Tutu (later Mpho Tutu Van Furth), he issued the Global Forgiveness Challenge and published *The Book of Forgiving.*[5] This offered 'a fourfold path for healing ourselves and our world', its four steps consisting of 'telling the story', 'naming the hurt', 'granting forgiveness' and 'renewing or releasing the relationship'. Alongside the familiar mixture of psychology, faith and politics was a political reach with the broadest possible compass – 'healing our world'.

This global healing aspiration was to be achieved by overcoming the hardwired or natural tendency to engage what they called the Revenge Cycle, and instead seeking to heal the self. Left to their natural dispositions, it was asserted, people choose the Revenge Cycle and seek to 'harm back', thereby opening the door to a series of negative and destructive consequences which eventually leads to 'revenge, retaliation, payback'. When this gets out of hand violence and cruelty result and yet more people get hurt. And as those people are also hardwired for retaliation the cycle inevitably repeats itself. Thus vengeful violence is understood to perpetuate itself, getting progressively worse, until someone presses pause to engage the Forgiveness Cycle and make space for their own need for healing – choosing to heal rather than harm, as it was put.

The decision not to retaliate but to opt for self-healing isn't the end of the matter, however. The next step is to 'tell the story'. This is followed by 'naming the hurt'. Only then do we get to 'granting forgiveness'. Then it is time to decide whether to renew or release the relationship; that is, whether to continue to engage with the forgiven harmer or walk away.

Absolutely fundamental to the Tutu approach to forgiveness is the African notion of *ubuntu* – 'I am because we are'. The emphasis is on the humanity and dignity of each person, whatever they have done, and the interconnectedness of all people. Indeed, recognizing the humanity of even the foulest perpetrator of horrendous actions is almost equated with forgiving them. Given that apartheid was based on a false, brutal and rigorously hierarchical categorizing of human beings, it is perhaps not surprising that the Tutu approach to forgiveness was grounded in the understanding that every human being has equal worth. His gospel of forgiveness was a very post-apartheid message: that it was of paramount importance not to dehumanize others – even if they were guilty of perpetrating horrendous and cruel harms.

But the Tutu line was not just about dignity: it was about potential. He profoundly believed that every human being could, given the opportunity, change for the better, and that this is why we should forgive rather than condemn someone on the basis of their worst actions in the past. And this is why it is better to forgive and hope for change than condemn someone on the basis of their past worst actions. This is evident in a section of *The Book of Forgiving* clearly written by Desmond, where he explains how in one very public case he felt a duty to speak out in favour of this belief in human dignity and the capacity to change.

Johan Kotze's crime was not connected with apartheid, but gathered a widespread notoriety and outraged many across South Africa. Given what he did, outrage and disgust feel natural and appropriate. Having seen his estranged wife Ina Bonette with another man, Kotze forced three (black) labourers to rape and mutilate her. After that he forced her to watch while he shot her son Conrad dead. The story generated a great deal of media coverage. When the retired archbishop saw the headline 'The Monster of Modimolle' he felt he had to take a stand, and wrote to the newspaper's editor that 'Mr Johan Kotze remains a child of God with a capacity to become a saint.'[6]

> Let us condemn ghastly acts, but let us never relinquish the hope that the doers of the most heinous deeds can and may change . . . The stories we heard at the TRC were horrific, some were bloodcurdling, yet we witnessed extraordinary acts of forgiveness as perpetrator and victim embraced and did so publicly. We believed then, and I still believe now, that it is possible for people to change for the better. It is more than just possible; it is in our nature . . . in each and every one of us.[7]

It is interesting that Tutu decided to intervene in this case, and significant that he leveraged, one might say, the TRC and the 'extraordinary acts of forgiveness'. He isn't asking anyone to forgive Kotze, and it is not clear that anyone else is seeing this as a dispute about forgiveness.

If they did, they might be asking what the immediate victims, not least Ina Bonette and the labourers he coerced into raping her, have to say on the subject. But Tutu references the heroic forgiveness of others because forgiveness had become for him the most profound, practical and impressive expression of two beliefs that were fundamental to his vision of how to move on from apartheid: a flat refusal to consider anyone as less than human whether as branding them a monster or in any other way, and a determination to hope that even the most evil of perpetrators might change.

The Tutus had a vision of globalized, healing and reconciling forgiveness, but how did they see the connection with Christianity? This question is directly answered in their book.

> The Forgiveness Cycle is a universal and non-sectarian cycle. Obviously, in [our] faith, our model of the ultimate example of forgiveness is Jesus Christ, who on the cross was able to ask forgiveness for those who were torturing and ultimately killing him. But forgiveness does not require faith.[8]

Desmond Tutu made it clear that there was nothing distinctively Christian about his understanding of forgiveness. There is some irony in this, given the extent to which others saw him as Christianizing a secular process by his clerical dress and demeanour and use of religious language in the context of the TRC, but that speaks to the complexity of the cultural and religious muddle that dogs so many attempts to engage with or apply forgiveness. Tutu contributes to this when he sacralizes forgiveness, even if it is in what he believes to be a 'non-sectarian' way. For instance, in his response to acts of forgiveness, seeing something spiritually impressive, or even holy, about victims who offered words of forgiveness. 'Let us take off our shoes,' he might say if forgiveness was sought or offered, 'for we are standing on holy ground'. This is a reference to the encounter between Moses and God at the burning bush in the biblical book Exodus, a pivotal moment not only in the history of the liberation of Jewish people from slavery in Egypt but also in black consciousness. This was all of a piece with describing Jesus as the supreme exemplar of a forgiving person. For Tutu, to forgive was in the best interests of any survivor of harm and integrally connected with personal healing, but also a particularly profound way of moving towards reconciliation and civil harmony. Forgiveness had never had such a good press. But equally it had never had such a politically and culturally intricate local expression, and it had never had so many expectations heaped upon it. Suddenly it seemed as if history turned on the magnanimity of the 'little people'.

Tutu achieved an astonishingly authoritative status as Christian prelate, justice campaigner, witness to suffering, reconciler supreme and champion of personal well-being, and used this to project his version of forgiveness. It is hard to imagine him as anything other than an archbishop, but had a celebrity psychotherapist, or perhaps a prominent lawyer and civil rights activist, been the chair of the TRC it is unlikely that their pronouncements on forgiveness would have had nearly the impact of Archbishop Tutu's. His words and work gave forgiveness a rocket-powered boost because he was a religious figure working for the creation of a new state. That he worked alongside the most potent political symbol of a forgiving disposition in the twentieth century, Nelson Mandela, increased the power of that message. Mandela himself said relatively little about forgiveness, but his stance was understood to be forgiving. It was widely noticed and remarked upon, for instance, that his gaoler for 20 years on Robben Island was given a seat of honour at his inauguration ceremony. Desmond Tutu was not presented as a forgiver himself, but as Chair of the TRC he became the primary emotional witness of stories of horrendous suffering and loss and then – almost without a breath – of stories of forgiveness, and thereafter the advocate-in-chief of forgiveness itself.

Desmond Tutu was a hugely important figure in the ending of apartheid and the relatively peaceful transition to democracy in South Africa. He was also in later life a powerful advocate of the rights of oppressed minorities, as well as one of the most impressive and influential clergy of his generation, and the most well-known. His charisma was to be funny and amusing as well as prophetic and powerful. However, there are serious problems with the way he put forgiveness on such a high pedestal and singled out those who forgave for superlative praise. And it is troubling to learn that in the TRC hearings pressure was put on victims to express forgiveness,[9] especially since those who appealed for amnesty had to show neither remorse nor regret or offer any kind of restitution. In a much more recent book Mpho Tutu Van Furth takes issue with the emphasis on forgiveness and amnesty in the TRC process, protesting that what was offered in a spirit of *ubuntu* was received in a spirit of individualism – 'So forgiveness for you was what set you free of all responsibility from us.'[10]

The voice of forgiveness in the 1990s became loud and strong not because Tutu presented to the world a more appealing Christian ethic towards enemies than did Provost Howard of Coventry in 1941, but because the mixture of the therapeutic and the political, the deeply emotional and the highly public, the symbolic and the representational, meant that ironically, perhaps, an archbishop's championing of forgiveness through and after the TRC projected forgiveness to a huge audience hungry for what it promised. Tutu witnessed many acts of forgiveness and solicited many more, mostly from poor black women. The people they forgave were torturers, beaters, rapists and murderers. And by and large these were men with jobs, homes, families, a place in the suburbs. Some would have been very glad to be forgiven in addition to receiving amnesty. And need it be doubted that many who observed from afar, and marvelled at the forgiveness being delivered, were monitoring this at a deeper level and thinking that a world in which the voice of forgiveness is powerful is a very good world for the rich and the secure, indeed for those with anything troubling their conscience?

One of Archbishop Tutu's most famous observations was that 'we may be surprised at the people we find in heaven. God has a soft spot for sinners. His standards are quite low.' That may be a great message during political transition, but the message lands differently in different contexts, as the fictional letters of Chapter 2 so bluntly convey.

Although a religious figure, Tutu was central to the projection of forgiveness beyond the religious sphere into the political realm. Christians delighted that he had drawn attention to the jewel in the crown of thorns. Forgiveness was good for victims, liberating for perpetrators and transformative of politics, exemplified by Jesus Christ on the cross and a very practical way in which human beings could emulate the qualities of God as merciful and compassionate. There are perhaps moments, personal and historical, where most of this can come together in a flash of charismatic transformation. But the idealization of forgiveness and forgivers is unrealistic and unsustainable. There is a shadow side to the promotion of forgiveness.

7

Christianity

Sarah Stewart Holland was a 16-year-old student at Heath High School in Paducah, Kentucky in 1997 when freshman student Michael Carneal opened fire on a prayer group, killing three. She arrived that day just after the shooting and, unlike most, entered the school and witnessed the carnage. The following day when the students came back to school Sarah joined those who made posters to place in the windows proclaiming their forgiveness of the killer.

> The fact that the shooting had happened during prayer circle seemed significant to me. I had often attended the early morning prayer meeting, and I felt both blessed I had been late that morning and guilty I hadn't been attending the prayer circle more regularly. My simultaneous feelings of guilt and gratitude manifested in a driving desire to forgive Michael Carneal. I went to the library and spent hours making signs with several of my classmates to display in the school windows.[1]

The signs carried messages such as, 'We forgive you Michael', and, 'We forgive you because God also forgave us.' One read, 'We can forgive but never forget', and another offered a mini sermon: 'When people genuinely turn to God no matter what kind of mess they've gotten into he responds with love + FORGIVENESS.'

The posters made a big impact. Stewart Holland was interviewed, Bible in hand, telling ABC News about how God's love enabled her to forgive.

Whether or not there was, or ever could be, any genuine forgiveness in those signs, there was certainly no closure. At the time Stewart Holland was peaceful, calm and composed, and felt this meant she was 'OK'. Subsequently she realized she wasn't. She had profound overreaction to any death and a terrible fear of losing loved ones when parted from them.

> Over a decade after the shooting at Heath High School, I went to counselling. After only a handful of sessions, my counsellor diagnosed me with post-traumatic stress disorder. She told me that the traumatic way I had been introduced to death as a teenager had left me with an unhealthy obsession with it.

In the article in the *Atlantic* in which she tells this story, Stewart Holland doesn't judge or condemn her 16-year-old enthusiasm for forgiveness. Nor does she question what right or standing she and her classmates had to speak out in this way. I cannot help agreeing with the American rabbi Danya Ruttenberg, however, who sees in this response the 'short-circuiting' of 'a process that may need to be longer, deeper and more complex than might feel ideal'.[2] I see no evidence that Stewart Holland was specifically pressured into forgiveness, but clearly she was making what she thought an appropriate spiritual response; that she was being a good Christian in leading the signwriting. And it is not unreasonable to imagine the forgiving high school students being offered as exemplars from pulpits across the land, reinforcing the sense of forgiveness that lay behind the teenage signwriting.

The idea that to be faithful Christians must find it in their heart to forgive those who harm them runs very deep. The theology professor and bishop Stephen Sykes began a book about the theology of the atonement, the understanding of how Jesus Christ reconciled sinful humanity to God, by quoting a victim of torture, whom he doesn't name, who was asked whether he had forgiven his Japanese torturers. 'I can't speak for everyone,' he replied, 'but as for myself, I am a Christian and therefore I should forgive.'[3]

When an attempt was made to assassinate Pope John Paul II, he was seriously and painfully wounded. But while he was still in the ambulance he resolved to forgive. It took two years before he could do so in person, at a famous though confidential meeting with Mehmet Ali Agca. The Pope would not reveal details of the conversation but said, 'I spoke to him as a brother whom I have pardoned, and who has my complete trust.' While many were impressed, no one was surprised that a Christian leader would forgive. Figures such as Cardinal Basil Hume of Westminster drew attention both to the pope's victimhood and his Christ-like forgiving spirit. 'He is now at one with the countless victims of violence of our day. He, like them, has now followed in the footsteps of a Master who was himself so cruelly and callously tortured and killed. He, like his Master, refuses to condemn, is ready to forgive.'[4]

It is easy to find statements from Christians advocating forgiveness, not only at the popular level but also in serious academic papers. For instance, in an article about forgiveness and reconciliation in Northern Ireland published in 2011, the Oxford professor Nigel Biggar mentions an occasion when, at a conference about forgiveness, reconciliation and 'burying the past', a woman stood up and questioned the whole premise of the event. She knew who had informed on her in the former East Germany; he lived in the same street and still did. She had no desire to reconcile and could see no point in seeking to forge any kind of relationship with the man: 'I didn't know him then and I certainly don't want to know him now.' So why even raise the question of reconciliation? 'I do it because I am a Christian,' Biggar answers.

> The obligation to forgive wrongdoers is a very prominent one in the teaching and example of Jesus; and Christians are therefore bound to consider what forgiveness requires, when faced with the business of righting wrongs. Talk of forgiveness is not unique to Christianity, of course, but it does seem to be uniquely pronounced there.[5]

Biggar is probably right that forgiveness enthusiasts can be found in most faiths and among people who have a secular outlook on life, but its association with Christianity is strong and contributes to the kind of respect and admiration given to forgivers. According to some thinkers and preachers it would seem that the notion of forgiveness has no limit; that nothing and no one is ever unforgivable. As we have seen, Archbishop Desmond Tutu was a strong advocate of forgiveness in the final decades of his life, and a central plank of his thinking was that no one should be written off; that each and every person, no matter what evil deeds they had done, was a child of God who might one day come to themselves and make changes in their life. To say that someone is unforgivable or to designate them a 'monster' was, for Tutu, to fail in hope and belief that a human being is made in the image of God – however tarnished or eclipsed that image has become.

Returning to Primo Levi, we might note that he concluded his thoughts on forgiveness by saying that, should a former persecutor change his attitudes and actions utterly and profoundly, then, in such a case, and only in such a case would he be 'prepared to follow the Jewish and Christian precept of forgiving my enemy, because an enemy who sees the error of his ways ceases to be an enemy'.[6]

If we go back to Charleston, we will realize that those who forgave Dylann Roof did not do so in response to any change of attitude on his part. He remained defiant in his hostile white supremacy. Indeed, it was the positive, unprompted, proactive nature of this forgiveness that was to many so impressive, and, for that matter, so Christian. For instance, in an op-ed in the *Washington Post* the following week Michael Gerson wrote that

> The killer was welcomed by the ones he murdered, and then forgiven by the people he deeply harmed. These victims and their families have shown what it

> means to be followers of Christ. And many of us now feel awed and honored to share the same faith as these remarkable Christians.[7]

The association between forgiving and Christianity is strong – but problematic. It has become necessary to pick this relationship apart and come to a more sophisticated and nuanced relationship between Christian ethics and the variety of meanings the word 'forgiveness' has today. But one point is abundantly clear: proprietorial and pushy as some Christians might be about forgiveness, it is absurd to suggest that only Christian theology properly understands or values forgiveness, or that only Christians are motivated to forgive or able to do so. Nonetheless, the myth of Christian exceptionalism when it comes to forgiveness has deep roots.

Charlotte Brontë's *Jane Eyre* is perhaps the most popular and widely read of nineteenth-century novels, and it returns to the question of forgiveness on several occasions. We have already seen Jane's silent forgiveness of Mr Rochester after he has tried but failed to enter a bigamous marriage with her. Much earlier in the novel, in Chapter 6, we come across a situation in which she is not forgiving at all. The child Jane sees another child, Helen, being treated badly by Miss Scatcherd. Helen is accepting, but Jane speaks out against behaviours that today would be considered abusive. 'If I were in your place I should dislike her; I should resist her; if she struck me with that rod I should get it from her hand; I should break it under her nose.' Helen responds that 'The Bible bids us return good for evil,' but Jane is not satisfied, and puts the case against forgiveness with precocious eloquence.

> If people were always kind and obedient to those who are cruel and unjust, the wicked people would have it all their own way: they would never feel afraid, and so they would never alter, but would grow worse and worse. When we are struck at without a reason, we should strike back again very hard; I am sure we should – so hard as to teach the person who struck us never to do it again . . . I must dislike those who, whatever I do to please them, persist in disliking me; I must resist those who punish me unjustly. It is as natural as that I should love those who show me affection, or submit to punishment when I feel it is deserved.

Helen thinks this a very inferior view, and a conversation ensues in which it becomes clear that Jane is not immediately persuaded by Helen's approach.

> 'Heathens and savage tribes hold that doctrine, but Christians and civilized nations disown it.'
>
> 'How? I don't understand.'
>
> 'It is not violence that best overcomes hate – nor vengeance that most certainly heals injury.'
>
> 'What then?'
>
> 'Read the New Testament, and observe what Christ says, and how He acts; make His word your rule, and His conduct your example.'
>
> 'What does He say?'
>
> 'Love your enemies; bless them that curse you; do good to them that hate you and despitefully use you.'
>
> 'Then I should love Mrs Reed, which I cannot do; I should bless her son John, which is impossible.'

Given just how fraught and difficult discussion about forgiveness can be, whether conducted within a family or in the public square or in religious or philosophical circles, it is remarkable how the basic shape of the issues is set out in a discussion between children in a popular nineteenth-century novel! That doesn't mean there is nothing to say about forgiveness today. It is a reminder, however, that the subject is not only controversial but also perennial. It's also difficult and relevant across a huge spectrum of circumstances. This alone should tell us that generalizations and ideals are likely to become unstuck in specific contexts and situations – when, that is, we attend to the humanity of those who have harmed and those who have done the harming.

Dianna Ortiz, whose appalling torture was followed by the suggestion that she forgave, was interviewed on NPR on Easter Day 1996 by Daniel Zwerdling, who engaged this myth as he probed into her feelings. 'Jesus taught that the foundation of spirituality and love was forgiveness,' he said, referencing the resurrection: 'Can you forgive the man who tortured you?'

Her response was that it was a very difficult question. 'I guess at this point in my life I'm not able to forgive,' she went on. 'I leave that in God's hands'.

Zwerdling pressed further, asking if she thought about it and 'wrestled with it'.

'I do, and the fact that I'm a Catholic nun and I'm not able to forgive, that makes me feel all the more guilty.'

The interview ends with her saying, 'I'm not sure what it means to forgive.'[8]

A far more confident approach to forgiveness is taken by the influential New York evangelical Tim Keller, whose book *Forgive* was published in 2022 just months before he died. In it he makes this trenchant point.

> If you believe the gospel – that you are saved by sheer grace and the free forgiveness of God – and you still hold a grudge – at the very least it shows that you are blocking the actual effect of the gospel in your life, or you're kidding yourself and perhaps you don't believe the gospel at all. Either way, spiritually speaking, to not forgive somebody is to put yourself in a kind of jail.[9]

That's pressure.

Rabbi Danya Ruttenberg is trenchantly against pressuring people into forgiveness, and writes that 'Forced and coerced forgiveness is not only toxic – it can be lethal.'[10] As evidence she cites that more than half of all female homicide victims are killed by an intimate partner. How many of them, she invites us to consider, had tolerated or forgiven abuse because of the generic pro-forgiveness nature of American culture?

Questions about the priority or appropriateness of forgiveness are of course being asked all the time. Few have expressed one of the most perplexing issues more clearly than the abused and neglected young woman, Kya, at the heart of Delia Owens' novel *Where the Crawdads Sing*, when she asks, 'Why should the injured, the still bleeding, bear the onus of forgiveness?' The question is one to which many might relate.

But forgiveness can also be presented extremely positively in contemporary America. As Ruttenberg puts it,

> It's regarded as a universal good, as something we should give, freely, regardless of whether the

> perpetrator of harm has done the work of repentance, regardless of whether they have fully owned their harm, regardless of whether they have done the work of repair, regardless of whether they have done the work of change.[11]

A tweet she quotes lays out the illogic of the fundamentalist Christian position: 'In my white, Christian, middle-class culture, not forgiving someone is seen as a bigger sin than the original action. It . . . calls into question whether you're "godly" enough.' Ruttenberg offers further examples: the bullied employee urged to 'forgive and forget' when the matter isn't dealt with; the abused wife rebuked for leaving by the friend who writes about 'the power of forgiveness'. It is clear that enthusiasm for forgiveness needs to be moderated by care and concern for the harmed.

8

Leadership

Christian leaders today often present an earnest enthusiasm about forgiveness. The current Archbishop of Canterbury has identified 'reconciliation' as one of the three priorities for his period of office, and has bemoaned the unforgiving nature of contemporary society. One of the more famous occasions on which he put forward this message was an ITV news interview when he was asked whether the public should have a forgiving attitude towards Prince Andrew; the context being the Prince's association with the convicted paedophile Jeffrey Epstein and that he had made an out of court settlement with Virginia Giuffre who claimed he had sexually assaulted her when she was 17. 'Forgiveness really does matter,' said Welby. 'I think we have become a very, very unforgiving society.' He went on to clarify that we should distinguish between 'consequences and forgiveness', indicating his view that processes of justice are not undermined by forgiveness. A later clarification from his office added that, 'Both [forgiveness and consequences] are essential elements of the Christian understanding of justice, mercy and reconciliation.'[1]

A good example of Welby's enthusiasm for forgiveness is seen in a short article he was invited to contribute to *Prospect* magazine, to offer a particular lesson for 2019. Welby decided to explain 'the power of forgiveness' and its importance.[2] 'Forgiveness' he wrote, is 'the process by which we recognize guilt, and yet release it.' In other words, the power of forgiveness is that it recognizes and affirms what is wrong – what is genuinely guilt-worthy, one might say – and yet moves on. 'Forgiveness accepts that harm has been done and that harm cannot be ignored,' as Welby puts it; 'for ignoring it opens the door to impunity and injustice.' At this point the Archbishop is approaching an insight into forgiveness found especially clearly in the writings of the Croatian Lutheran theologian Miroslav Volf, now based at Yale. Volf formulates forgiveness as an 'exclusion' of sin and 'embrace' of the sinner, and emphasizes that someone can only be forgiven *after* they have been judged to be culpable. To forgive is not to rescind a judgement, find an excuse, downgrade a crime or to brush off the wrongness of how one has been treated. It is to make a second judgement after the first. To forgive is to say what happened was wrong and outrageous and has caused terrible and perhaps irreparable damage – but . . . I *nevertheless* forgive. 'To forgive is not to pretend that nothing has happened,' explained Welby: 'it is the opposite. It accepts the full weight of wrong, looks at it, considers it, weighs it and then dissolves it through grace and love.'

Forgiveness has the quality of 'nevertheless', or 'but' or 'and yet', about it. What you did was wrong. And it was harmful. Nothing is ever going to change that. And yet I forgive – I let it go. I no longer hold it against you. The way forward after forgiveness is shaped but not constrained by the judgement that the harming action was harmful and wrong. It is the culpable who are forgiven, but they remain culpable. This (I think) is what Welby means when he says that forgiveness does not eradicate consequences. The slate, so to speak, is not wiped clean. To some Christian ears this will sound at least a little odd, because they have been brought up on the idea that wiping the slate clean, or cancelling the debt, is precisely what forgiveness does. But Welby is right: there are limits to what forgiveness achieves. There's a time for 'but' and there's a time for 'and'.

The problem with Welby's article, however, and his approach more generally, is that in his enthusiasm to promote forgiveness as means of preventing the development of hatred and violence can sometimes obscure the distinction between forgiveness and tolerance. These are compatible, but one is not the other. Welby sometimes muddles us by putting a gracious and tolerant approach towards those with whom we disagree on the same footing as a forgiving response towards those who have harmed us. The reason he does this is because for him everything is framed by reconciliation. That's the priority, the main goal. And people are unreconciled, alienated or at odds with one another for a variety of different reasons which, unfortunately, his reconciliation paradigm fails to distinguish between clearly enough. This is connected with his observation that in our culture today many people are affronted and offended, or even angered or enraged, by those who disagree or have different personal, social, ethical or political values and priorities.

Welby is undoubtedly right in noticing the shrill tone of public life and the intolerance of those who fail to conform with certain modes of thought, not least in areas where politics and identity combine, or in his own domain of religion. But his conflation is unfortunate and potentially misleading. Forgiveness is involved in some serious mission creep if we use it as a word to describe both the process of recognizing guilt and then releasing it *and* as the everyday politeness of being respectful and tolerant of those who hold different opinions and views to our own. While not wanting to be held to this or any other definition I can see that it is reasonable to say that forgiveness is releasing the guilt from someone who has done wrong; but it is unhelpful to confound the suspension of judgement necessary to sympathetic understanding, with forgiveness. Forgiveness is relevant to those who have been harmed, not those who have been disagreed with. It is harms and wrongs that can be forgiven, not irritations.

Welby's enthusiasm for forgiveness is the mirror image of his concern that we are becoming an unforgiving society. He knows that forgiveness can be transformative, so its absence is as tragic as its presence is wonderful. 'I spend a great deal of my time in places where the absence of forgiveness leads to an ever-more destructive cycle of retribution, hatred and vendetta,' he writes in his *Prospect* article. 'Yet I also see, in some of these places, the capacity of those who have suffered more than I can begin to imagine, to forgive.'

Welby is right that forgiveness can 'break the cycle of violence' – a real insight in respect of civil war or terrorism, where one atrocity leads to an even worse reprisal. It is one of the threads of the Tutu forgiveness mission, and intellectually goes back to Hannah Arendt's observation that forgiveness can interrupt history by breaking the problem of irreversibility. One of the attractions of forgiveness to those looking to spiritualize life is that it seems to come in at an orthogonal direction to time's arrow, stopping it in its tracks and preventing escalatory consequences when it looks as though they are the inevitable next step.

To the eyes of faith such forgiveness will be the grace of God connecting with and transforming situations where violence is not so much cyclic as spiralling out of control. But spirals of violence are not the only sadness in town. And again, context and details really do matter. Domestic violence may be cyclic, but not in the sense intended here. It's not fuelled by retaliation so much as habit and repetition. Systematic racism may have its seasons, but is not fuelled by tit-for-tat responses. The abuse of the vulnerable doubtless has patterns, as the predatory abuser prowls on to identify their next victim, but the issue here is not that payback gets out of hand or that retribution is excessive. There is too much power differential, too much manipulation and control for that. In a situation of conflict driven by a reprisal mentality Welby's forgiveness is absolutely what is needed. In other situations, however, it might be absolutely what is *not* needed.

There is another fly in the ointment of Welby's forgiveness, and it is a very typically Christian one, as we shall see. For the model of forgiveness here is 'unconditional'. It does not depend on the attitude of the one who has inflicted the harm. In all these regards the Archbishop represents very well an approach to forgiveness that is contemporary and Christian. The problem with it is that it takes as its starting point not the impact of harm and the needs of the wounded or violated but the overall priority of reconciliation. To be sure, there are times when forgiveness, sometimes heroic forgiveness, can be offered as a contribution to a reconciliatory process, but there are also times when the victim's needs must come ahead of the aspirations of the wider community. Failure to understand this lies behind some of the problems the Church has had in dealing with the clerical abuse of those under its care. It is not the same as the problem of putting the risk of reputational damage ahead of the need for honest acknowledgement, but it can have similar consequences. The reconciliatory paradigm, it seems, requires the idealization of forgiveness and the idolization of forgivers. And as such it inevitably adds to the burden of people like Chris Green.

Another enthusiastic promoter of forgiveness was the hugely prolific and influential minister of Westminster Chapel in London for 25 years until 2002, R. T. Kendall. For him forgiveness is about eradicating every last trace of negativity. The word 'total' is fundamental to Kendall's teaching. His book is called *Total Forgiveness*, and he writes about 'a total cessation of negative feelings towards the offender'.[3] Interestingly, and perhaps surprisingly, Kendall sees reconciliation as a lesser consideration, and strongly counsels those who attempt or achieve total forgiveness *not* to let the person they have forgiven know. For him forgiveness is vitally a matter of the heart, and we can therefore equally well apply it to the dead as well as the living. It has nothing whatsoever to do with the attitude of the offender towards the offended, and is not impacted in the least by their subsequent behaviour towards the offended or others. It is the utter and gratuitous eradication of anger, hatred, bitterness, grievance – anything that might clutter the inner being of the harmed person.

In the final chapter of his book, Kendall gives examples of how the totality of forgiveness might be achieved when repeated prayer is not effective. One is of 'a lady in her forties whose father had seriously abused her', who retained a spirit of heaviness despite telling God in prayer how she had forgiven her father. She was counselled not only to forgive him but also to bless him. This she did, and the results are said to have been immediate and astonishing. According to an eyewitness she 'went ballistic', the spirit of heaviness departed and the lady herself reported some weeks later that her life was 'completely changed'.[4]

Canon Stephen Hance, now the Church of England's Director of Mission, and formerly a cathedral dean, has edited a substantial book about forgiveness that takes a not dissimilar view to Kendall.[5] Forgiveness, he stresses, doesn't mean minimizing the seriousness of the offence; rather it is 'an act of handing over responsibility for judgement to the one who is able to carry that responsibility and to exercise it wisely, so that my [the one who has been harmed's] own sense of peace and well-being might be restored'.[6] The idea is that responsibility for judgement and response to one's harm is handed over to God.[7] He tells a story which, remarkably like Kendall's, is of a woman who could not forgive her father – though this father seems to have been negligently rather than actively abusive. Again there is talk of struggle in prayer, and while the woman could pray for her father in various ways she could not bring herself to forgive him until . . . she did. Then 'the impact was immediate. A new lightness came upon her, and over the next weeks and months it stayed with her.'[8] The point of the story is that the woman's life was improved, as well as her relationship with God – which was understood to be less than it might have been because of her inability to forgive her father. For Hance 'this kind of forgiveness is essentially about inner peacemaking.' The harm inflicted by the father is acknowledged and addressed within, but the father is not held to account or challenged. He does not have a chance to give his side of the story, or perhaps to apologize and learn the lessons and do what he can to put things right; indeed, the whole range of possibilities regarding the relationship with the father are seen as utterly irrelevant to forgiveness.

Another influential Anglian priest, the vicar of St Martin in the Fields in London, Samuel Wells, has also recently offered his understanding of forgiveness. In a book called *Love Mercy* he introduces his 'twelve steps of forgiveness'. In the introduction, Wells explains that the first six of his steps, here described as steps of peace, are not necessarily theological but that steps seven–ten (seven being forgiveness itself) are explicitly Christian and 'involve specific Christian practices that seek to imitate the ways of the Trinity'.[9]

Turning to Chapter 7, we find it opens with the following sentence.

> Forgiveness is a decision by one or more parties not to be defined by resentment and antagonism, to seek a bigger life than one constantly overshadowed by this painful story, and to allow one's perception of the harm received no longer to stand in highlighted isolation but to blend slowly into the myriad of wrongs and griefs to which the world has been subject across time.[10]

Forgiveness here has three parts, each with its own verb. To decide, to seek and to allow. The wording is nuanced and carefully avoids being too categorical. It would seem from what Wells has written that some resentment and antagonisms might remain after forgiveness, though they are no longer 'defining'. The forgiver also seeks – but may or may not achieve – a 'bigger' life than one overshadowed by whatever happened. And finally, there is the most complex part of the definition, which might be understood either in terms of *reframing* the harm in a larger context or *remembering* it differently. Either way, it is a psychological adjustment to limit the ongoing impact of the harm on the harmed.

We seem to be in very different territory here from Welby's forgiveness as the release of guilt for the sake of reconciliation, Kendall's total elimination of negative feelings or Hance's pastoral facilitation of inner peace.

Other Christian leaders offer further perspectives on forgiveness. The Church of England Bishop of Chelmsford, Guli Frances-Dehqani, has a particular reason to speak about forgiveness and a distinct authority in doing so. She was born in Iran where her father was bishop, and lived there until her parents were forced to move away – her father exercising his ministry in exile. When Guli was still a child her older brother Bahram was killed by the authorities, a terrible loss to the family. In a published Good Friday address on forgiveness, she quotes a prayer her father wrote for Bahram's funeral in Isfahan, which has become known as 'the Forgiveness Prayer'. The prayer, which was composed and read in Persian, must have been difficult to write, pray and speak at the service. Its burden is that God will forgive those who murdered Bahram on the day of judgement, pleading in their defence that the fruit of the spirit liberated by 'their crime' has caused the bereaved 'to follow more closely your footsteps in the way of sacrifice'. For Bishop Frances-Dehqani this 'defines forgiveness as the thing that enables us to trust more completely'. 'Forgiveness frees us from hatred,' she continues, 'allows us to love and releases us from the anxiety of our own death'.[11]

An approach to forgiveness remarkably different in presentational style, but perhaps with similarities to Kendall's and Hance's, is offered by the American Lutheran pastor Nadia Bolz-Weber. Appreciating that the emotions triggered in us in response to having been harmed can serve to attach us to the very person who harmed us (sometimes called trauma-bonding), she argues that we can forgive by severing this 'chain' of connection. This 'bolt-cutter' forgiveness involves intentionally putting aside thoughts and feelings that the person who has harmed us can continue to elicit from us, while not changing any of our judgements about them. Such forgiveness, she emphasizes, does not involve condoning what has been done, or capitulating to those who harm us. Bolt-cutter forgiveness might be a useful tactic in situations where those who have inflicted grievous or traumatic harm are not only unrepentant but in denial; where the task is, as she puts it, to forgive an asshole.[12] The point is not that they are pardoned; their slate is not wiped clean. It is excision of the person, not their exoneration. They remain guilty, and you still hold what they did against them – you just don't care enough about them for this to be an effortful or meaningful part of your life.

As Bolz-Weber makes abundantly plain in her video, bolt-cutter forgiveness is not an act of niceness or 'a pansy way of saying "It's OK."' It is 'an act of fidelity to an evil-cutting campaign' which prevents the victim from absorbing negativity from the event and from the perpetrator. This is the sort of forgiveness that is possible and perhaps necessary when the offender's attitude is such that it is impossible to summon up goodwill towards them or to find anything positive in them by way of regret, repentance or restitution. Its advantage is that it is not an unthinking reaction to the harming events, mirroring them and playing into the script of retaliation and escalation. Forgiveness is about being a self-freeing freedom fighter. Bolz-Weber is not quite unique in this sort of approach. The author Treva Draper-Imler once heard someone say that forgiveness was a matter of 'wishing that rotten SOB peace and getting on with your life'.[13]

My reading of the various ways in which Christian leaders promote forgiveness today, and the meaning of their public statements, is that Christianity is proud of its reputation as a religion of forgiveness and serious about promoting it as a force for good. It therefore encourages people to forgive, and is inclined to see a spiritual or theological aspect to forgiveness. Christianity celebrates and promotes exemplars of forgiving. However, it sometimes gets itself into something of a bind, as do other religions that promote forgiveness, as it wants to see it as a laudable, virtuous and spiritual action – while at the same time not the preserve of any kind of elite, but rather open to each and every person who has been harmed in any conceivable way in any possible circumstance.

Theology weaves in and out of Christian understandings of forgiveness in interesting ways. For Justin Welby it is part and parcel of the big narrative towards reconciliation; for Samuel Wells it reflects the inner life of the Trinity; for Kendall and Hance it is something connected with personal spirituality and intensity of prayer that aims at peace of mind. For the Bishop of Chelmsford forgiveness leads to trust, and for her father, the late Bishop of Iran, it involves seeing consolation beyond grievous loss and wicked injustice. Nadia Bolz-Weber is interested in self-liberation, and doing what one personally can to cut across the path of evil, which in turn perhaps connects with Welby's conflict-calming approach, except that reconciliation in any temporal sense is the last thing that 'forgiving an asshole' suggests.

There is a lot going on here, but I think it reasonable nonetheless to indicate some of the fundamental features of these variations on the Christian promotion of forgiveness. First, there is a recurrent overestimation of the relevance or reach of forgiveness, owing to its being confounded and confused with related virtues such as tolerance, patience, compassion and considerate attention to difference. Secondly, Christianity expands and confuses the category of *unconditional* forgiveness while sidelining what is often called *conditional* forgiveness. It ignores those forms of forgiveness that do in some way depend on the ongoing actions and attitudes of those who have harmed. This can be for well-meant and kindly reasons, and thus contemporary Christian teaching on forgiveness often reflects a psychological and therapeutic approach based on the notion that it is good for the victim/survivor to rid themselves of emotions and attitudes such as resentment, anger and bitterness because they are self-limiting and self-damaging. Part of this goes back to the work of Lewis Smedes and the psychological wing of the forgiveness industry of which Desmond Tutu was the patron saint. Certainly we now live in an era when many see interpersonal forgiveness as a free and independent act of the individual and not as a response to a change in the person who inflicted harm.

Enthusiasm for forgiveness is certainly part of the rhetoric of pastoral practice of the Church today. This makes it difficult to give due consideration to the potential for a shadow side to forgiveness, not least in the extent to which it can create pressures on the harmed to see it as the priority. It is true that in recent years a plethora of statements have stressed that forgiveness is not a duty and that no one should be pressured into forgiving. Nonetheless, there is a gap in the Christian promotion of forgiveness where we might expect to find praise of at least some forms of unforgiveness, openness to the possibility that forgiveness has real limits, and a recognition that it might be appropriate sometimes to conclude that we are in the realm of the unforgivable.

This is not a new suggestion, of course; just not a very Christian one. The Shoah, in which over six million Jews were killed in an unparalleled project of genocide, has itself been described as 'unforgivable' by twentieth-century philosophers and others. The French philosopher Vladimir Jankélévitch famously argued that France should not follow West Germany's example in introducing a 20-year statute of limitation for those who have perpetrated crimes against humanity, on the grounds that they are 'inexpiable'. What happened in the Shoah, he goes on, was 'an assault against the human being as a human being, not against such and such a person, inasmuch as they are this or that'. As a result, 'pardoning died in the death camps.'[14]

Hannah Arendt's judgement that the trial of Adolf Eichmann revealed 'the banality of evil' has sometimes been taken to mean that she was underestimating the impact of evil acts. She was not; rather saying that atrocious consequences come from the aggregation of many low-level decisions and actions. But her account concludes with as clear an understanding as possible that she did not see any scope at all for his forgiveness.

> For politics is not like the nursery; in politics obedience and support are the same. And just as you supported and carried out a policy of not wanting to

share the earth with the Jewish people and the people of a number of other nations, as though you and your superiors had any right to determine who should and who should not inhabit the world, we find that no one, that is, no member of the human race, can be expected to want to share the earth with you. This is the reason, and the only reason, you must hang.[15]

9

Karl

It is perhaps hardly surprising that it is a book about the Shoah that has generated one of the most wide-ranging discussions of forgiveness. I refer here to Simon Wiesenthal's *The Sunflower*. The book consists of two sections. In the first, Wiesenthal recounts an incident that occurred while he was incarcerated in a Nazi concentration camp, and what it prompted him to do after the war. The second part of the book, the 'Symposium', consists of responses to the book from prominent thinkers, all of whom were invited to say whether they thought Wiesenthal had responded well, and what they thought they would have done in his situation. The book was first published in English in 1976, and the most recent edition contains almost 50 responses. It has been extremely widely read and discussed and remains a challenging and complex text to respond to, both because of the narrative's central dilemma, and because of the divergence and strength of views in the various responses in the Symposium.[1]

In his memoir, Wiesenthal explains how a dying SS officer had had 'a Jew' (himself) summoned to his bedside so he could tell the story of his participation in a massacre in Dnipropetovsk (now Dnipro), Ukraine, and ask forgiveness. This officer, Karl, had been raised as Roman Catholic and was familiar with the idea of confession and absolution, but sought forgiveness not from a priest but from a representative of the Jews. The nature of his confession was detailed and horrific. Hundreds of Jews had been crammed into a house, some of them forced to take cans of petrol with them, which was then bombarded with hand grenades and became an inferno. The SS officer was clearly now full of guilt and remorse, deeply troubled both by what he had witnessed and by what he himself had done. He particularly remembered a man whose clothes were alight who held a small child at a second-floor window and then jumped with her into the street. 'We shot,' he confessed. Then he continued, 'I don't know how many tried to jump out of the windows but that one family I shall never forget – least of all the child. It had black hair and dark eyes . . .'[2]

Later the officer makes his request.

> I know that what I have told you is terrible. In the long nights while I have been waiting for death, time and time again I have longed to talk about it to a Jew and beg forgiveness from him. Only I didn't know whether there were any Jews left . . .[3]

His voice trails off. Wiesenthal reflects for a while on what he's heard and then, 'At last I made up my mind and without a word I left the room.'[4]

Had Wiesenthal been entirely comfortable with his restraint he may never have written his story up as *The Sunflower*. But telling his story was not enough to put his mind at rest. He felt his silence was at the very least debatable, and ended his narrative with these words.

> Was my silence at the bedside of the dying Nazi right or wrong? This is a profound moral question that challenges the conscience of the reader of this episode, just as much as it once challenged my heart and my mind . . .
>
> The crux of the matter is, of course, the question of forgiveness. Forgetting is something that time alone takes care of, but forgiveness is an act of volition, and only the sufferer is qualified to make the decision.
>
> You, who have just read this sad and tragic episode in my life, can mentally change places with me and ask yourself the crucial question, 'What would I have done?'[5]

The circumstances in which Wiesenthal found himself were extreme, and some of his respondents declined to think that they could, at a distance, develop a sense of how they would respond. Others thought that, despite being asked, it would be inappropriate to respond, and some, such as Jean Amery, dismissed the whole notion of forgiveness as irrelevant. The British journalist and publisher Mark Goulden came to the conclusion that 'I would have silently left the deathbed having made quite certain there was now one less Nazi in the world.'[6]

A number of the correspondents were academics or teachers, among them Eva Fleischner, who reports that she has often used the text in her Holocaust course, and that it has frequently led to animated discussions. My own experience of introducing students to the text is also that it engages them deeply. One once told me it had given her a sleepless night.

'Was that the description of the massacre?' I asked.

'No,' she said, 'it was wrestling with the dilemma.' She got really locked into the multiple ways of considering and answering Wiesenthal's questions, constantly seeing a different side as she tossed and turned throughout the night. Fleischner, however, reports something different.

> One striking feature of these [animated discussions] has been, that, almost without exception, the Christian students come out in favour of forgiveness, while the Jewish students feel that Simon did the right thing by not granting the dying man's wish.[7]

This division is also reflected in the responses recorded in the Symposium. Bishop Desmond Tutu made it clear that he would have followed the example of Nelson Mandela and those who offered forgiveness in the course of the TRC hearings. He also mentioned the example of Jesus on the cross. 'Forgiveness', he concluded, 'is not some nebulous thing. It is practical politics. Without forgiveness, there is no future.'[8]

Rabbi Abraham Heschel, on the other hand, made the opposite position equally clear.

> No one can forgive crimes committed against other people. It is therefore preposterous to assume that anybody alive can extend forgiveness for the suffering of any one of the six million people who perished.
>
> According to Jewish tradition, even God Himself can only forgive sins committed against Himself, not against man.[9]

My own engagement with *The Sunflower* began in Prague in the early 1990s. Through the helpful offices of the anthropologist Professor Ernest Gellner I had arranged a visit soon after the city was liberated from Communist rule, and was able to meet a variety of fascinating people and ask for their perspectives on the agendas for change, reconciliation and forgiveness that might be developing. I am sure my questions must have been naïve and annoying, but they were met with courteous responsiveness. An American journalist at the English language newspaper, the *Prague Post*, asked if I had ever read *The Sunflower*. I hadn't even heard of it, but since then I have often returned to it and found it a source of continuous challenge to my thinking.

Since that first reading, however, I have felt that Simon Wiesenthal acted with integrity and that his response was proportionate and wise. He had shown kindness and consideration; had declined to view the dying man as 'just another Nazi'. He had not said, 'Absolutely I do not forgive you! I hope you roast in hell.' He had not put a pillow over Karl's head and savagely snuffed out the remainder of his life. Indeed, for me one of the important aspects of this story is not so much 'forgiveness' itself and when it may or may not happen, as the recognition of the humanity of one who has clearly and evidently behaved in a way that denied, undermined and brutally terminated the humanity of others. I still think Wiesenthal's demeanour and attitude towards Karl was humane and compassionate. And I don't think it would have been a better response to the request had he said, 'Yes, as a Jew I forgive you.'

The fundamental mistakes here, and the reason why this became an anguished tale about forgiveness, lie with Karl. Wiesenthal's only error, it seems to me, is in allowing Karl to frame the encounter as a potential forgiveness story that might or might not reach its conclusion. Karl's mistakes matter not so much because one dying Nazi soldier made them, but because they reveal fundamental misunderstandings hardwired into the way those influenced by Christian doctrine, liturgy and culture try to deal with the aftermath of harm.

So what are Karl's mistakes?

To be completely clear, I am not talking about Karl's life choices in joining the Hitler Youth movement or the SS or in participating in a massacre. Rather the question is, what are the options for someone who finds himself in such a situation, tormented by the recollection of his own acts and the suffering he knows he was active in inflicting. A trauma-aware reading of *The Sunflower* might today suggest that this dying man was suffering from post-traumatic stress disorder, but Karl would not have been thinking in such terms, and it was his Roman Catholic formation rather than mental health considerations that came to the forefront of his consciousness as he lay on his deathbed.

What Karl thought he needed was absolution. Absolving, like everything else in the forgiveness word-pond, is not a straightforward or uncontested concept. Nonetheless, it is reasonable to suppose that he had been taught that when he confessed his sins to a priest he would receive absolution. He would have longed to hear the words '*Ego absolve te*' – I absolve you. This practice is not unique to Roman Catholicism, but in Catholic teaching confession is apt preparation for receiving either Holy Communion or for death. It is absolution which returns the sinful soul to a 'state of grace'. This is what Karl longed for. Some would consider it as a holy desire and that he genuinely wanted to be at peace with God ahead of the journey of death, which he would understand to lead to divine judgement. Others might feel that it was fear-fed and narcissistic.

This, then, was Karl's first mistake. He wanted to put his sins in the past so he could approach God with his head held high for blessing. You don't have to agree with me, but I invite you to wonder whether absolution is an appropriate or in any sense praiseworthy desire on the part of someone who has participated in the brutal murder of innocents and given his adult energies to the violent imposition of Nazi ideology. Confess, and then for ever in heaven? It at least makes you question how happy a gathering that eternal communion might be – particularly if Desmond Tutu is right and 'God has a soft spot for sinners.'

We know that Karl decided not to go to a priest to confess, but made the idiosyncratic decision to find 'a Jew', a representative of the people he had harmed. There is, if I can put it this way, something *almost* admirable about this deeply flawed strategy. Unfortunately for Karl the flaws are fatal, but let me explain first what I mean by 'almost admirable'.

What I think his decision to confess to 'a Jew' represented was the intuition that what he had done wasn't reducible to being nothing more than a sin against God. That might seem more than obvious, but the reality is that there are plenty of people who have gone to confession in such circumstances. This is something that has come to light as the child abuse crisis in churches has been investigated and soundly criticized, and for some calls into question the whole practice of confession. Whether it has led the practitioners and enthusiasts for confession themselves, especially in churches where it is voluntary, to change their minds is not so apparent, with enthusiasts for confession often arguing that it is not primarily abusers but the abused who seek consolation in confession. However, the abuse crisis has done nothing to soften long-held reservations about the practice; that there is something not quite right about dealing with matters of actual harm against others by means of an intensely spiritual conversation conducted in a hyper-confidential space, with the so-called legal 'Seal' of the confessional prohibiting the confessor from sharing, using or disclosing that information to anyone else.

The good intuition in Karl of wanting to confess to 'a Jew' is that whatever it is that might free Karl from the guilty torments he is experiencing needs to involve those who were his victims. What he failed to understand, though, was that in approaching 'a Jew' he was approaching someone whose religious tradition had decisively closed the door on the course he was pursing. It is the point made by Rabbi Heschel and many other commentators: that no one can forgive on behalf of the dead. 'Forgiveness to the injured doth belong,' wrote John Dryden, words many will sympathize with. Just a moment's thought will see the commonsense in them. If a person who has been harmed discovers that the person responsible confesses their guilt and remorse to a third party who duly forgives, they are likely to be further offended. You break my window, but my cousin in the next street forgives you . . . that *can't* be how it works.

Judaism is very plain about this, and also about God not being able to forgive interpersonal injuries. This theology is written into the understanding and words of prayers at Yom Kippur. It follows that when the victim is dead there can be no forgiveness. This does not denote a lack of goodwill, compassion or empathy. Nor does it suggest that hatred is being harboured or revenge plotted. It is, you might say, a technicality. No living victim, no forgiveness. End of conversation.

This approach to the forgiveness of those who have committed murder, however, does not seem to have the natural support of commonsense or casual observation. In fact, there are many stories of bereaved parents forgiving the murderer of their child, and some of bereaved children forgiving their parent's killer. Indeed, post-mortem forgiveness is one of the largest categories of stories on the Forgiveness Project website, and many memoirs have been written by those who have forgiven murderers. Would it be right to suggest that these bereaved parents are wrong to think that they have forgiven when they clearly believe they have? Worse still, does it mean that by purporting to have forgiven they have done something wrong? Surely that would be too harsh. To be clear, I believe that to forgive is a possibility for those who have been bereaved by murderous actions. I do not, however, believe that such forgiveness adds up to pardon or absolution.

There is a weird asymmetry in forgiveness that is sometimes forgotten, and has its origin in the sad truth that every harming action can have many consequences – cause many harms. So a person may, and it's obvious once you think about it, be both forgiven and unforgiven for the same action. By summoning 'a Jew' instead of a priest, Karl therefore created two unresolvable problems. The first was asking a Jew to forgive on behalf of the dead. The second was thinking that a representative human being could fill the symbolic and ritual space occupied by a priest – the representation of Christ – in the sacrament of confession and absolution. These are excruciating mistakes to make, and important because they show just how difficult it is to have a coherent theology of this practice.

There is a further problem. Karl's action reflects the very mentality that informed and shaped the whole Nazi project. He sent for a Jew – any Jew – and had him led to his bedside; a venture fraught with danger for whichever Jew was selected. Everything about the way in which he went about this reinforced the point that 'the Jew' was less than human, merely useful to Karl, an item to be used. This is something to which the Christian commentators on Wiesenthal's story seem largely insensitive. It is a very odd oversight, and cannot be explained by saying it is a subtle or debatable point. It isn't. It is absolutely and plainly part of the narrative. It can only be accounted, I think, to the Christian tendency to take the side of the harmer when it comes to matters of forgiveness. A perpetrator bias such as some have suggested is hardwired into Christian thinking about forgiveness.

You can see this among the Christian responses in *The Sunflower*. For in some cases – and remember the story takes place in a concentration camp – there is an overriding desire to ease the burden of the perpetrator, a predisposition to accept whatever he has offered as a sign of sincere remorse or repentance and to meet that with what he has asked for. As the Roman Catholic priest Edward Flannery explains in his response, 'It is a cardinal principle of Judeo-Christian ethics that forgiveness must always be granted to the sincerely repentant. The only seeming exception . . . is in the New Testament allusion to the "unforgivable in against the Holy Spirit".'[10] He concludes by saying that in Simon's place he hoped he would have forgiven and,

> as an obstinate believer, suggested to [Karl] that he make peace with God by asking for his forgiveness and, taking full advantage of the situation, uttered a prayer for the repose of his soul and those of the victims of his inhumane behavior.[11]

The Archbishop of Vienna had this to say about forgiving when one is not oneself a victim.

> Even though an individual cannot forgive what was done to *others*, because he is not competent to do that, there is still a question of whether one *may* forgive. For Christians, the binding answer is in the Gospels. The question of whether there is a limit to forgiveness has been emphatically answered by Christ in the negative.[12]

He concluded that for Wiesenthal to have delivered 'an explicit' pardon under the circumstances 'would have surpassed our concept of the human'. Addressing Wiesenthal directly, he nevertheless suggests that 'the fact that you did not take advantage of this opportunity may be what still haunts you as a striving human being.'[13]

I find the different position taken by a Roman Catholic priest who has engaged extensively in

Catholic-Jewish relations, Eugene Fisher, much more realistic and helpful. Fisher sees Wiesenthal's question as anticipating a tension in Jewish-Christian relations – with some Christians impatient to see something more like forgiveness emanating from Jewish sources with regard to the Shoah. He takes a contrary view.

> It is the height of arrogance for Christians to ask Jews to forgive them. On what grounds? We can, as established by evidence of changed teachings and changed behaviour, repent and work towards mutual *reconciliation* with Jews. But we have no right to put Jewish survivors in the impossible moral position of offering forgiveness, implicitly, in the name of the six million . . . Placing a Jew in the anguished position further victimizes him or her. This, in my reading, was the final sin of the dying Nazi.[14]

In his view, Christian discomfort at a lack of Jewish forgiveness is in effect 'a sad replay of the ancient stereotypes that had contributed to the problem in the first place'.[15] Also, he distinguishes, to my mind both accurately and helpfully, between expressing repentance and asking for forgiveness. This seems to me a vital distinction if well-meaning enthusiasm for forgiveness is not to become pro-perpetrator bias and a device for cementing the oppression of the oppressed, the exploitation of the exploited and the abuse of the abused. I develop this significantly in the second section.

I have offered an unusual reading, *The Sunflower*, by concentrating on the mistakes that Karl made when he appreciated the full horror of his position as a perpetrator. But Karl's position is important to critique because, as the response of Eva Fleischner's Christian students, and at least some of the Christian contributions to the Symposium suggest, it is one that gains Christian sympathy. To me this reflects a Christian mindset that offers excessive scope to be narcissistic and exploitative. Karl had the right idea when he recognized that to seek absolution through sacramental confession to a priest was not appropriate, but in summoning 'a Jew' to be his confessor things went from possibly good to worse. For all his Catholic formation, Karl completely lacked the ethical, spiritual and human imagination to work out what might be appropriate. Simon Wiesenthal, on the other hand, responded with admirable humanity and compassion. He also drew the line in the right place, before forgiveness.

10

Jesus

In his recent book on forgiveness, the scholar and episcopal priest based at Harvard Memorial Church, Matthew Potts, has aptly written that 'New Testament forgiveness is a slippery thing, to say the least.'[1] This is partly because, despite the high premium placed on forgiveness by many Christians, and Christianity's reputation as a religion of forgiveness, there is, as the British New Testament scholar, ethicist and Anglican priest Professor Anthony Bash has put it, 'astonishingly little' in the New Testament about it. That observation has not prevented him writing two books and several academic papers exploring that 'astonishingly little'. There may not be much of it, but it is not at all straightforward to interpret or apply.[2]

One of the issues we face is that Jesus wasn't a philosopher and never defined his terms. There is no, 'Forgiveness is . . .' or, 'By forgiveness I mean this and not that' in the New Testament. Nor did he ever sit down and say, 'Now I want to share with you my wisdom regarding how you should behave when you have been harmed or offended by the actions of another person – in particular I want to explain to you what I mean by the word *forgiveness*.'

Four gospels tell the life and teaching of Jesus, but two of them have hardly anything to say about forgiveness. These are Mark, the shortest and first to be written, and John, the last to be written and in some ways the most sophisticated. In fact, the one time forgiveness is mentioned in John it is in the context of Jesus's post-resurrection visit to his disciples, when he breathes the Holy Spirit on them and says, 'If you forgive the sins of any, they are forgiven them; if you retain the sins of any, they are retained.' (John 20.23) Which, to those who have imbibed the myth of Jesus and forgiveness, is probably a shock to the system. According to that myth Jesus should have said, 'Whosoever's sins you forgive, they are forgiven, and whosoever's sins you retain, they will *in any case ultimately be forgiven.*' However, he didn't; he put the possibility of unforgiveness on the table at the very moment when he breathed the Spirit on to the apostles and commissioned them for mission. Just as when God spoke to Moses on the mountain top and promised to be 'forgiving iniquity and transgression and sin, yet by no means clearing the guilty'. (Exodus 34.7)

Then there's the question of translation. Jesus spoke Aramaic, the Gospels were written in Greek and we speak contemporary English. That leaves lots of scope for meanings and nuances, association and connotations to be lost, or added, in translation. Inevitably, then, we must consider the vocabulary: the New Testament Greek word-pond. First we should note that the verb translated as 'forgive', *aphiemi*, occurs quite often in the New Testament, but isn't usually translated as 'forgive'. It carries meanings such as 'let go', 'liberate', 'free from' or 'release'. It has a geographical or spatial frame of reference, and literally or metaphorically means something like 'put a distance between'.

By the way, this is the word used when Pontius Pilate asks the crowd to choose between Jesus and Barabbas. It was in Pilate's power to 'release' one of them. Interestingly, no Bible translation uses the word 'forgive' in this instance. That's perhaps understandable, but if any were to use the word 'pardon', that would not be inconsistent with how the word is used when, for instance, the President of the United States exercises that peculiar constitutional power.

The equivalent noun, *aphesis*, is also found in the Gospels, but there are far more instances of the verb than the noun – which is the opposite, in my observation, of much contemporary writing about 'forgiveness', where the noun predominates over the verb. I suspect this focus on the verb in the Gospels is because the gospel writers, like Jesus, were not very much interested in theories or abstractions, but rather in acting and doing and making a difference and getting things done. But what does *aphesis* refer to? It is not fair to think that at the time of Jesus the word *aphesis* would have had exactly the same meaning and usage as 'forgiveness' does in English today. And this should encourage us to be cautious. In particular, the word is about releasing someone or something.

In the epistles a different word is translated as 'forgive': *charizomai*, which suggests not 'release' but 'giving'. The plain meaning of the word in the New Testament is to give or grant, but it also sometimes implies undeserved kindness. This aspect of forgiveness is reflected in contemporary European languages, and in English, French and German it's in the second syllable:

for-GIVE, *par-DONNER*, *ver-GEBEN*. This connection between forgiveness and giving has been developed by Christian theologians to stress that forgiveness cannot to be earnt or deserved, and that therefore to forgive is to act generously or, as some might say, graciously; the implication being that this is not only good or virtuous in human terms but also in some deep way reflects the nature of God, or is even the grace of God flowing through a human being.

We cannot derive a contemporary spirituality or ethics of forgiveness from these brief word studies. But it is helpful, I think, to appreciate the extent to which even the vocabulary of forgiveness itself is textured, nuanced and complicated – and built on metaphors. Then we can perhaps appreciate why it is that dealing faithfully and well with the aftermath of harm will not be resolved by reading the Bible as if it were simple and clear about these matters. The words themselves rule that out.

Turning to the gospel books, we begin with Mark, and note that it opens not with Christmas stories but with John the Baptist 'proclaiming a baptism of repentance for the forgiveness of sins' (Mark 1.4). The prioritizing of repentance is something Christianity has found it very hard to hold on to – but here it is at the very beginning of the oldest gospel we have. We will return to this in Chapter 11.

Most of what Mark has to say about forgiveness thereafter concerns God's forgiveness, its connection with healing and Jesus's authority to declare it. There is very little on interpersonal forgiveness, apart from this one verse: 'When you stand praying, if you hold anything against anyone, forgive them, so that your father in heaven may forgive you your sins.' (Mark 11.25) – a broad statement that relates to the Jewish idea that you should seek to be reconciled with your neighbour before seeking reconciliation with God.

This is only one verse, and we might note that Luke has a very similar, but importantly different one: 'If your brother or sister sins against you, rebuke them; and if they repent, forgive them. Even if they sin against you seven times in a day and seven times come back to you saying, "I repent," you must forgive them.' (Luke 17.3–4) Here there is pressure to forgive, but this is not forgiveness that comes out of nowhere: it is the forgiveness of those who have harmed *and repented*. This reflects rabbinic teaching that has remained decisive in Judaism. It is not about unconditional forgiveness.

There is possibly another difference between Mark and Luke. In Luke, the instruction refers to someone who has sinned against you. In Mark there is no clarification that what is being 'held against' someone is in anyway justified. The point might just be that if you are trying to pray and someone is dominating your thoughts, then – let them go. You could be ruminating about them for all sorts of reasons. Envy, perhaps, or because you are over-reacting to a minor offence. Certainly to take that verse from Mark as meaning that when someone has harmed you grievously you must quickly and thoroughly release your resentment and sense of justice needing to be done is to read a huge amount into the text. It would be more reliable, I suggest, to stick with Luke's idea that if you have been harmed the next step is for the harmer to repent.

Earlier in Luke's gospel Jesus gives a short lesson in how to behave towards your enemies. We should do good to them, he says: bless them, pray for them, turn the other cheek to them, give to them and let them take from us. That's an interesting list of activity and passivity, and certainly very challenging. It makes me want to know more about what Jesus means by 'enemy'. I suspect this teaching is intended as indicative rather than prescriptive; the main point being that we should work out how to *love* our enemies in situations where they are or become actively hostile, and try to come up with actions and attitudes consistent with loving them.

It is interesting and important that 'forgive' is not on Jesus's list as recorded by Luke. Samuel Wells tells us that this is because Jesus is talking about hatred, abuse and violence that are still current. 'To forgive something that is still going on', he asserts,

> is a category mistake . . . Forgiveness has to wait until the activity is over. You can't forgive something that's still going on, because that seems to be saying that what is going on is the whole story and therefore that it's somehow acceptable.[3]

There's lots to think about there, and in Chapter 15 we will take a closer look at the question of forgiving in a context of ongoing hatred.

It is Matthew's gospel which gives the clearest support to the myth that Jesus states that God requires absolute unconditional forgiveness under all circumstances. It is in Matthew's gospel (only) that Peter asks Jesus how many times he should forgive his brother if he sins against him, suggesting up to seven times. Jesus replies not seven, but seventy times seven. (Matthew 18.22)

Jesus loved to use hyperbolic statements. What he meant was – just keep forgiving. It's not a matter of counting.

Matthew then leads into the story often referred to as the Parable of the Unforgiving Servant (Matthew 18.23–35), in which someone who has been let off an enormous debt will not release a poor man from a very minor one. The use of the word 'unforgiving' might suggest that this is the kind of situation which today might prompt a discussion about forgiveness – that is, a story of one person who has harmed another. But that's not the case. It would be better if it were called the story of the Ungenerous Servant. Or the Mean, or Rapacious Servant. All that is – or rather isn't – forgiven is a financial debt. The 'unforgiver' is the one who does not release a poor man from a financial obligation that will ruin him. And this in the context of the lender having just been released from an overwhelmingly enormous debt.

To be released from a debt is different to being forgiven after having inflicted grievous harm through doing wrong. And to move from a debt release story to a forgiveness-after-harm imperative seems to me unjustified. But many have argued that the word 'debt' doesn't only have the literal meaning that you owe money, but is also a biblical metaphor for sin, which makes the parable about more than debt relief. This is a reasonable point, and the parable does suggest that there is an important relationship between God's forgiveness of sins and the interpersonal forgiveness of offences and injuries. Nonetheless I do not think it can reasonably be read to suggest that God requires those who have been subject to life-changing and traumatic harm to 'forgive' – as if the request to forgive in such an instance is trivial in comparison with the forgiveness that God bestows upon a sinner. What I think *does* follow from the parable is the clear teaching that if one is subject to relatively trivial infringements, inconveniences or indignities, or for that matter annoying and yet not deeply life-changing harms, then it is appropriate to see them in the context of life's ups and downs. In such a situation it is right not to hold on to your indignation, but rather to take the wider view that we all need to be forgiven, and appreciate that it is good to be generous towards those who are in some small way indebted to us.

The Christian tradition, well understood, encourages people to bring a sense of proportion and perspective, and indeed subjectivity, to their moral judgements. The reality is that some debts really are minor, and we can live with them perfectly well. Nothing much is at stake, and society and community, indeed any kind of relational life, is impossible unless people maintain a light touch in interpersonal debt-keeping. The point here is to be positive in forgiving the easily forgivable.

I read the connected 'seventy times seven' passage in the same way. That Jesus so exaggerates tells me that he was talking about low-level offences, irritations and provocations – interpersonal sins, the like of which we are all very familiar with, and frequently. They require us to take a breath and find that mixture of tolerance, benevolence and hope that allows us to make the situation good. Today I forgive you, yesterday you forgave me and tomorrow – who knows?

The subheading in the New Revised Standard Version of the Bible refers to the *Unforgiving* Servant, but we should remember that these subheadings were not written by the evangelists. Check out the King James or Authorized Version if you don't believe me; they are absent from that classic document because they are a more recent addition. They are guides to the reader by modern editors, and have no more status than that. If it were down to me, the subheading for this section would refer to the Parable of the Mean Servant. The overall message of the seventy-times-seven answer and the parable is, 'Don't sweat the morally small stuff; learn how to live with life's irritations.'

We also have to deal with the Lord's Prayer, where we are accustomed to read, and pray, 'Forgive us our trespasses/sins as we forgive those who trespass/sin against us.' This needs careful handling. The stakes are high.

In Chapter 2 I mentioned an appreciative email from someone I am calling Jennifer who had read my book *Healing Agony*, following which we had a fruitful exchange. Here is a further extract from what she wrote to help me understand where she was coming from.

> A child is abused by her father. In that moment she loses her innocence and her trust. She tells her mother, who hits her and calls her evil, and a great many other things as well. The child has now lost her healthy ego and gained a sense of sin that takes hold forever. The child then goes to church and says the Lord's Prayer. 'Forgive us our trespasses,' she says, thereby acknowledging her sin, and then, 'as we forgive those that trespass against us', thereby dismissing her pain and shock in eight short words.

Jennifer wrote this in the third person, but she was that child. And she has told me that, although she experienced debilitating shame and guilt for decades, even at that stage in her life she had a degree of determination and, somehow, she steadfastly held on to the knowledge that she *wasn't* sinful and was not, therefore, going to ask for forgiveness. She was not responsible for the abuse she experienced (from her parent) and did not allow herself to feel guilty about it. However, these complex dynamics created 'a barrier between her and Christ, which she couldn't and wouldn't break'. As she put it, 'it is no wonder that the child struggled for much of her life with the idea of sin and Christianity. And forgiveness.'

At one level the question is whether the child was getting the message that Jesus intended. Is the meaning of the Lord's Prayer that in dealing with the worst things that happen to us we have to get to a point of forgiveness before we can hope that God would be forgiving towards us?

You know the answer is going to be 'no', but let me give you some reasons.

First, the words 'trespasses' or 'sins' are in this context not a translation of the standard Greek word for sins, but the standard Greek word for 'debt'. So we are in similar territory to the parable of the mean servant, and I would make a similar point. This is not about the big stuff. It's about trespasses. Little things – 'misdedeis' or 'misdeeds' were the words used in a twelfth-century English version of the prayer. In the fourteenth century John Wycliffe reverted to 'debts', and in the sixteenth century William Tyndale introduced the word 'trespasses' – which we might think of as missteps. Whichever way you look at it, this is not about life-changing or traumatic harm. It's not about abuse, oppression or exploitation. If it is about sins, it's about small-'s' sins, not capital- 'T' traumas; it's not about torture, rape or murder.[4]

Secondly, wouldn't it be a bit arrogant and un-prayer-like to offer oneself to God saying, 'Ahem, I have now forgiven that evil SOB who defrauded me, the wicked woman down the street who is forever telling lies about me, and even my hateful old dad who went berserk when I came out to him and then never spoke to me again. Now, dear God, it's your turn to forgive me.' No, that really doesn't stack up.

The 2017 Church of England booklet *Forgiveness and Reconciliation in the Aftermath of Abuse*, commenting on both the Lord's Prayer and the parable of the ungrateful servant, puts it like this:

> The lesson for the disciples is not that 'unless you forgive, God cannot forgive you,' which would make God's mercy conditional on our actions; rather that in response to God's abundant mercy we should be forgiving to those who ask us for mercy.[5]

That's helpful, though I'd prefer to use the words 'generous' or 'merciful' or 'loving' in place of the word 'forgiving'.

A really crude translation of the phrase in question in the Lord's Prayer might be, 'Release us from our debts – as we also have released those indebted to us.' So it might be better to take a broader approach and to see this as meaning, 'Be generous towards us, as we are generous towards others.' Such generosity to others could take positive and negative forms: a kind of kindness on the one hand and a kind of mercy on the other. This I believe is always going to need to be interpreted in a given situation, but it is consistent with loving one another in the sense that the biblical scholar Nicholas Wolterstorff has described as 'care-*agape*'. *Agape* is one of several different Greek words translated as 'love' in the New Testament. It is not only forgiveness that has translation issues.

Wolterstorff distinguishes care-*agape* from benevolence-*agape*, which is indulgent and pays no attention to any harsh or demeaning or disrespectful behaviour. Care-*agape*, on the other hand, is love for others that seeks to see them justly treated and flourishing.[6] If we see Jesus's prayer as a means of connecting human and divine love it follows that we cannot exclude the flourishing of the harmed, or the claims of justice, from its forgiveness clauses. Victims and survivors need to learn how to pray it without fear that it forces them to forgive when forgiveness does not serve flourishing or justice. Whatever forgiveness is it cannot be a contradiction of care-*agape*.

Another way of opening up space for humanity in this tense clause is to wonder what the pre-Greek Aramaic version of the Lord's Prayer might have meant to those who first prayed it. Neil Douglas-Klotz has suggested that the original Aramaic might have been translated as, 'Loose the cords of mistakes binding us, as we release the strands we hold of others' guilt.' The advantage of this is that it shifts the mind from the worrying territory of apparent absolutes and binaries: forgive – yes or no, and you will be forgiven – or not, to the imagery of cords and strands, which are held tightly or loosely. This seems far more sympathetic to the experience of those who are entangled in the 'web of sin' – a phrase I coined when trying to explore the way in which we are trapped by our own sins.[7] Douglas-Klotz's version affirms the connectedness between what we need from God – help with the entanglements of sin in which we find ourselves, and what we can offer others – help with their entanglement, without one being presented as the condition or price to be paid for the other. Additionally, spiritual pressure to forgive fails to recognize that victims and survivors might have other ethical responsibilities – such as speaking out not only so that perpetrators might face justice but also so that others may not be harmed.

We all need help to be freed from the unhelpful entanglements caused by our less good choices, and the consequences we had never intended, and we often gratuitously hinder the freedom of others by keeping hold of the strands of their guilt. But if we read this Lord's Prayer petition in the knowledge that when Jesus commissioned his disciples he did not instruct them to forgive everything, and instead implied that they should sometimes release and sometimes retain, then we might be best advised to apply that advice to ourselves.

The notion that Jesus was relentlessly forgiving, and requires us to be indiscriminate on our forgiving, really doesn't stand up. Jesus encouraged a broad generosity of spirit, and outlined the sort of contexts in which this might be 'cashed out', in stories where meanings are blended and in hyperbolic answers to questions. But his message was never, 'Thou shalt always forgive, and if thou dost not thou shalt not be forgiven,' and no one should pretend that he did. Why? Because when forgiveness is simplified and over-promoted it's the abused, the harmed and the exploited who pay the price and suffer the consequences.

Another observation that might be helpful to those still burdened by forgiveness-anxiety is that the nature of the harm determines not only whether or not forgiveness might be appropriate but also the relationship between the harm and the harmed. It is one thing for a parent or a king or another powerful authority figure to forgive someone who has offended or hurt them. It is quite another for the junior, weaker, less powerful person to forgive the one who has abused their power. Forgiveness up is different to forgiveness down, and both are different to peer forgiveness. These nuances are relatively under-explored in teaching and theorizing about forgiveness, but are integral to situations where harm is inflicted by the abuse of power.

I have left this point to last, but it is a hugely important dynamic in the Gospels, and in line with Jesus's overall message and mandate to bring 'good news for the poor'. The word 'poor' might mean those without material wealth, but more profoundly it means those with less power, the vulnerable. And when we say vulnerable, we mean in this context the potentially and actually abused, the potentially and actually oppressed, the potentially and actually exploited.

At its worst Christianity, and indeed the understanding of forgiveness it is partly responsible for and certainly associated with, looks to the weak to absolve the strong, and to the harmed to exonerate the harmer. It puts pressure on the justifiably angry to release their indignation before its cause has been properly addressed. It is absolutely clear, however, that the gospel of Jesus is not about putting pressure on the abused, exploited, oppressed or otherwise harmed to give a free pass to those who inflict harm on them. His message is certainly that they should not retaliate. But that does not mean that 'all is forgivable' or that 'all should be forgiven.' If anything, Jesus seems to model non-retaliatory anger.

The other myth we need to consider is whether Jesus was himself a habitual forgiver, and whether he forgave those who were putting him to death as he was dying on the cross.

First, was he a habitual forgiver? My answer is, 'No, but it's hard to prove a negative,' so I leave it to the reader to think of an occasion. To help, here are some scenarios. One of the disciples does something that harms Jesus personally. They then see that this was bad, feel remorse, apologize, say it won't be repeated. Jesus then says, 'That's fine, I understand. Don't worry about it.'

You don't recollect that from the Gospels, because it isn't there.

Or how about: Jesus, still a teenager, goes to the temple and chats to the elders, and tells them he's really mad with his parents because he feels they're neglecting him in subtle ways, for instance insisting he does menial tasks in the workshop instead of studying the scriptures or exploring the countryside with his friends. They are even patronizing enough to tell him it's too dangerous to be out alone with the Roman soldiers in occupation. Two of the elders shake their heads. 'You know,' they say, 'that's what it's like to be young,' but the third takes Jesus to one side and says, 'I can feel your pain and distress. It's good that you've shared it. Let's now go through a process I've devised which will allow you to release that anger and resentment. You'll feel so much better for it.'

You don't remember that either. Jesus *did* talk to the elders in the temple, and it seems his parents didn't notice he was missing when they got back home, so their parenting might sometimes have been a bit dubious, but as to what he discussed with the elders we have no idea. I am confident it would not have been about whether the best way to deal with any negative feelings towards parents would be to forgive them.

The point of these examples, of course, is to show the absurdity of imagining anything like the psychological, relational process we now think of as forgiveness being present in the life of Jesus.

There is no evidence that Jesus was an active, prolific forgiver in any of the contemporary senses of the word. We might further observe that he wasn't much of a reconciler either. I once heard a tremendous sermon at St Mary's Episcopal Church, Manhattanville, which serves the West Harlem district of Manhattan, New York, that railed against reconciliation. 'I am not a reconciler,' thundered the preacher: 'I am an *advocate*!' And he had easy pickings when it came to finding 'proof texts' that suggest that, rather than being a reconciler, Jesus was intent on causing conflict. 'I have not come to bring peace but a sword,' for starters, not to mention Jesus's comments about turning family members against one another. Another line I recall is that 'the only people Jesus reconciled were Pilate and Herod': a very awkward and often unnoticed verse in the gospel of Luke. Let me quote it in context.

> And when [Pilate] learned that [Jesus] was under Herod's jurisdiction, he sent him off to Herod, who was himself in Jerusalem at that time. When Herod saw Jesus, he was very glad, for he had been wanting to see him for a long time, because he had heard about him and was hoping to see him perform some sign. He questioned him at some length, but Jesus gave him no answer. The chief priests and the scribes stood by, vehemently accusing him. Even Herod with his soldiers treated him with contempt and mocked him; then he put an elegant robe on him and sent him back to Pilate. *That same day Herod and Pilate became friends with each other; before this they had been enemies.* (Luke 23.7–12)

This is a reminder that abstract notions are not always ethical notions. We can reconcile, or collaborate, for that matter, and 'release' for a variety of reasons and with a variety of results. The same is true of physical items, of course: a hammer can be a carpentry tool or a murder weapon.

A more positive Biblical reconciliation takes place after Jesus's resurrection when he encounters Peter at the lakeside. Just as Peter has denied Jesus three times before, so Jesus asks him now three times whether he loves him. Peter answers in the affirmative with increasing vehemence, and Jesus commissions him to lead his followers. Was this a good move on Jesus's part? Of course. But it wasn't easy or quick or unconditional. We know that Peter was immediately filled with remorse when he heard the cock crow – he went out and wept bitterly. The little conversation with Jesus doesn't accept remorse as enough, but wants a statement of friendship and love – interpersonal commitment. Peter needs these questions and the opportunity to answer them to help him become both forgivable and open to being forgiven.

The truth, perhaps, is that our human processes of emotional and moral repair, the exchanges that allow us to let go of the past, reassemble our integrity and summon up the dignity and poise to face the challenges of the next stage of our life, career or vocation, don't necessarily fit naturally under the categories of our nouns and verbs. This is why I am increasingly cautious about making too much of the power of these words. To do so can make it seem as if 'forgiveness' is something that itself has agency and power. I can see it as an informal figure of speech, and it would be great if 'forgiveness' could just enter the room, or the spirit of reconciliation be at large in our community. But these are ways of talking about the odd chemistry of values and capacities and character; anything less idiomatic risks becoming an inappropriate and therefore misleading reification. Nor am I an enthusiast for building plans for action on abstractions. There is no such *thing* as forgiveness. There are only people who forgive. Or who don't forgive. There is no such thing as reconciliation. There are only people who do or don't reconcile – and they may do so for good or bad reasons with good or bad results.

And finally, did Jesus forgive those who killed him? The evidence for this comes from one verse in Luke's gospel – which in fact only appears in a few of the earliest manuscripts and reads, 'Father, forgive them, for they know not what they do.' (Luke 23.34) Countless people have referred to this as Jesus forgiving his killers. The current Archbishop of Wales even wrote in a Lent book he produced for his diocese that Jesus 'commanded us to forgive even as he hung on a tree'.[8]

I think I can be quite succinct and plain about this. It was a prayer. It was directed to God. It wasn't an act of forgiveness. It wasn't the opposite of forgiveness, nor was it an outburst of anger or a cry for revenge. These words from the cross constitute a beautiful and hugely impressive and commendable utterance, and whenever they are read or heard they have a great impact. But what is the right impact, the correct interpretation of this prayer? My suggestion is that it is most effective in opening the space where mercy and kindness might flow in the midst of cruelty, horror, violence and the whole gut-wrenching mess of Golgotha. In fact, I would say that the words are diminished by interpreting them as something as improbable and unrealistic as a general forgiveness for – well, for whom? – the deserters, the betrayers, the temple authorities, Pontius Pilate, the bystanders or the soldiers? Or perhaps all of the above. Or everyone who has ever beheld a crucifix.

Jesus's short prayer wasn't an act of forgiveness, but it was impressive and important. Think of it as a final verbal contribution from a guru who teaches by allowing his prayers to be overheard. As so often, it's the context that matters. We are talking here about betrayal, abandonment, stripping, mocking, beating, nailing and hoisting up high, leading to excruciating pain of every kind, unresolvable dehydration and slow but terminal pressure on the chest to prevent breathing. We can understand the prayer of abandonment from the cross that Matthew and Mark record. Jesus reaches to the Psalms and prays, 'My God, my God, why have you forsaken me?' and we certainly understand him crying out in thirst. That he sought to unite his mother and his beloved friend is indicative of a real practical human love and compassion. The word that John records as his last, *tetelestai*, is ambiguous and challenges translators, commentators and preachers. Is it 'It is finished' or 'It is completed', or 'It is accomplished'? If so, what is the 'it'? But the prayer that they might be forgiven – released – by God from the sin of the act is all of a piece not with a life project of offering personal forgiveness whenever harmed, but of being the mediator of the forgiveness of God. That same instinct is perhaps revealed when Jesus addresses the so-called penitent thief: 'Today you will be with me in paradise.'

But no, Jesus didn't offer forgiveness from the cross, and he certainly didn't command anyone to forgive from that unlikely pulpit. It is one of several myths that have grown up and which exaggerate the importance that forgiving has in Christianity.

We may want to ask questions about this. For instance, although he didn't forgive, would it not have been better if he had? Might not a more Christ-like Jesus have declared forgiveness from the cross rather than handing the issue on to his Father? My response is that such questions themselves derive from the myth of Christian forgiveness as something that is always possible and always superlatively good. The reality, as I repeatedly claim here, is that there really are limits to the possibilities of forgiveness of every human being, and that recognizing these limits is fundamentally important to respecting and supporting those who have been harmed. For those who have suffered life-changing harm it is the Christ on the cross, who registers the need for forgiveness *and* does not achieve or deliver it, who can save them.

A far more sympathetic and useful and ancient Christian myth is that after Jesus descended into hell, he 'harrowed' it before bringing the departed with him to new and risen life. My suggestion here is that the harrowing of hell began not after he gave up the ghost, but while he was yet on the cross. When he said, 'Father, forgive,' and not 'I forgive,' Jesus opened a positive path for all who have suffered the unforgivable and proved that he was the Saviour of the abused, the exploited and the oppressed.

II

MOVING FORWARD

11

Repentance

Which of these is the better definition of forgiveness?

> *The release of resentment towards someone who has harmed you.*

Or,

> *The release of resentment towards someone who has repented of the fact that they have harmed you.*

You will have noticed the difference. It is 'repented'.

We are going to go behind the scenes of the word 'repentance'. Like forgiveness it can be a divisive word, but the division, at least sometimes, follows fairly predictable lines. There are those who think 'repentance' is irrelevant when it comes to forgiveness, because forgiveness is something a harmed person does completely independently of the attitude and actions of the harmer. For others, to forgive without repentance is a recipe for relational, ethical and social disaster. If you want to be a doormat, then you forgive everyone who treats you as one. It is philosophers and Jews who are inclined to take the view that repentance is important.

Psychologists and Buddhists consider it to be irrelevant. Christians appear on both sides of the divide, though most we have encountered so far have apparently been of the view that repentance is not relevant to forgiveness of one person by another; I take the contrary view that repentance is extremely important and, while not essential to every act of forgiveness, is extremely important when it comes to the limits of forgiveness and the question of forgivability.

To understand why philosophers and psychologists are on different sides of the line regarding repentance we need to look at how they approach forgiveness, and what they understand 'resentment' to be.

Psychologists and philosophers themselves tend to differ in their approach to forgiveness. A psychologist is concerned with the mental health and well-being of their client. A philosopher has no particular individual in mind, but investigates questions of logical coherence, meaning and purpose and, when it comes to forgiveness, brings the concept into play with other values, in particular 'justice' and other ethical considerations.

The idea that forgiveness is fundamentally about letting go of resentment held towards the person who harmed you has been very prominent in recent years. It is by no means the only release-based or letting-go-based way in which one might think about forgiveness, of course. There are those who would take a more behavioural view and say that it's about not retaliating or engaging in retribution. For others, words like 'hatred' encapsulate what they avoid or give up when they forgive. There are other words and thoughts too. For some people, to forgive is to no longer blame or subject to punishment. For others, to forgive is to no longer hold something against someone or to wipe out a moral debt.

In both psychology and philosophy, however, reflection on forgiveness has for some while been dominated by the question of resentment, though the two disciplines don't see resentment in the same way. Essentially, if a psychologist comes across a person who carries resentment, they will be concerned because they see it as a toxic and self-harming emotion. For a psychologist therefore resentment is something to be removed, eradicated, discharged or otherwise released, before it can do the poor person who is infected by it any further damage. For a psychologist, to be resentful is a fundamental aspect of the self-toxifying condition of unforgiveness. And in psychology unforgiveness has had a very bad press.

A philosopher would see resentment differently. In ethical thinking, resentment is an emotion of self-protection and self-respect. We defend our vulnerability and dignity, the thinking goes, by reacting with the emotion which tells us that what has happened is not only painful and hurtful but also just *wrong*, and that we should not put up with it. Resentment therefore has a job to do. Like physical pain it is a goad to action in our own best interest, such as taking our hand out of the flame. Also like pain, which doesn't stop as soon as the hand is out of the flame, resentment doesn't disappear as soon as the harm ends. In the aftermath of harm comes reflection, and if the harm is life-changing a whole raft of questions about responsibility and blame naturally follow. Removing resentment, therefore, is not the same as alleviating pain. Or so a philosopher would argue. It's not caused by simple hurt, but by hurt that should not have been inflicted and for which someone else is to blame. And until that 'should not' is addressed, that resentment will stay where it is.

Let's unpick the nuance in this. Every injurious action has two components. First, there is the behavioural or material aspect – we are needlessly kept waiting, we have something stolen from us, we are injured by someone's reckless behaviour, we are passed over for promotion in favour of someone less able because of some bias in the system. These sorts of things all harm us, but in parallel with the obvious harm there is another, and that is that in the process we are insulted. We resent because we notice the insult, and we know that if we don't feel and respond to it then no one else will. As the philosopher Jeffrie Murphy put it, 'Wrongdoing is in part a communicative act, an act that gives out a degrading or an insulting message to the victim – the message, "I count but you do not, and I may thus use you as a mere thing."'[1]

My own view is that the psychologists and the philosophers are both right about resentment. Yes, it is an emotion that tells us when we have been insulted or our vulnerability exploited, and yes, it acts as a poison in our system. I also think, by the way, that 'resentment' is only a word, a convenient label for a wide variety of emotions, including different sorts of anger and indignation and maybe some shades of disappointment and contempt, and a feeling that has been described as 'moral hatred'. These sorts of responses sit alongside physical and verbal ones, including various species of retaliation: hitting back, whether petulantly or in an act of planned revenge, or speaking back, whether as an instant rebuke or as a more considered and developed protest. To keep this relatively simple, assume that resentment is the inner human response to noticing and feeling the injustice and insult of being mistreated. And that, while resentment serves a good purpose, it can also be bad for us, and drive behavioural and verbal responses like retaliation and vengefulness.

So what should a victim do with their resentment?

Say there are two possibilities. Let it go – or let it act. The psychologists will prefer the 'let it go' approach, fearing that if you do not, then you will become more of a victim through the impact of resentment on you. The philosopher will prefer you to retain your resentment, to let it do its job of protecting you and maintaining your self-respect and dignity. Otherwise you will become more of a victim. Clearly both perspectives are important, but it is the philosophical approach which needs the concept of 'repentance'. Repentance here refers to actions the harmer might perform that mean the harmed person can forgive without becoming yet more vulnerable to harm and losing their self-respect.

The reasons people of different religions are on different sides when it comes to repentance are related to those that divide psychologists from philosophers, but include deep historical and theological dimensions. Repentance is originally a religious term. The question of repentance is from the Jewish perspective fairly straightforward, but from the Christian point of view repentance has a very strange and somewhat unfortunate history. The deepest core meaning of the word translated as 'repent', *teshuva*, is to 'turn'. The message of the prophets was that the people needed to turn from their wicked ways and return to the way, path or law of God. It was seen as the word to describe the return to a right and good relationship to God, but has since been applied to the question of what a person who has injured or harmed another person should do. For centuries many great and practical minds have sought to understand and explain what repentance means in the aftermath of human harming. We will get to that in the next chapter.

In Christianity 'repentance' obviously has the same deep taproot in the Hebrew word *teshuva*, but the New Testament was written in Greek, in which the word for 'repentance' is *metanoia*. This word does not have the connotation of literal or physical turning but refers instead to new knowledge, or different thinking, or, we could say, seeing and appraising things differently, or having a 'change of heart'.

In the fourth century, when Jerome translated the Greek New Testament into Latin he introduced a word that had connotations of neither turning nor new thinking but of receiving punishment or doing penance. That prisons in the United States are called 'penitentiaries' is no accident: it reflects Jerome's word choice when translating the Bible from Greek to Latin. In Scotland there is an old tradition of having a special seat called the 'stool of repentance' at the front of the kirk, on which known fornicators should sit for a period of shaming. It was Jerome who introduced the idea of punishment into the Western concepts of penance and repentance, but it is not fundamental or intrinsic to the biblical notion.

The Latin Bible was a hugely influential book, and those who created modern bibles by translating it into European languages tended to follow Jerome's example, so that, rather than the word 'repentance', readers would come across the word 'penance'. This, coupled with the practice of sacramental confession, meant that when someone approached God for forgiveness, they would have to confess their sins and receive and accept or 'do' a 'penance'. Working out which penance was appropriate for which sin became a whole sub-industry that learned priests would carry out on behalf of the others, and the penances they devised were known as tariffs. But accepting your punishment as a 'fair cop' or paying your tariff is completely different from taking responsibility and seeking to find the practical actions that will go some way to making amends and turn your life around.

The story doesn't end there, however, because when the Dutch polymath Erasmus was working on his translation of the New Testament, he identified this as a mistake and introduced the word 'repentance'. This was taken up by Martin Luther, who subsequently wrote to a friend,

> I learned – thanks to the work and talent of the most learned men who teach us Greek and Hebrew with such great devotion – that the word *poenitentia* means *metanoia* in Greek; it is derived from *meta* and *nous*, that is, from 'afterward' and 'mind.' *Poenitentia* or *metanoia*, therefore, means coming to one's right mind and a comprehension of one's own evil after one has accepted the damage and recognized the error. This is impossible without a change in one's disposition and love.[2]

More recent approaches, even in Catholic theology, have sought to get back to a deeper understanding of repentance. The scholarly English Franciscan priest

Fr Alban McCoy put it this way in a recently published sermon.

> It is obvious but bears repeating that God is not a scolding schoolmaster or a pushy parent. He doesn't want even our best effort; in fact, he doesn't want from us anything at all. He wants us. Repentance is the realization, in a rush of inexpressible and irrepressible relief, that we haven't chosen him: he's chosen us. It does, of course, involve turning away from our sins, but that turning away is a corollary and consequence of turning towards God's beauty and goodness.[3]

It would be hard to find a way of thinking that is more distant from the narrow idea of penance as punishment. But what Fr McCoy is more profoundly alluding to here is the Christian understanding that it is not human repentance that leads to divine forgiveness, but divine forgiveness that leads to human repentance. This is sound post-Augustinian Christian orthodoxy. Nothing comes before the grace of God, and the only human action that is relevant in the divine human relationship is human engagement in that grace – first receiving it, then responding to it and reflecting it forwards. The grace of God is, and creates, the ultimate virtuous circle.

However, what this reveals, once again, is that taking God's forgiveness of sinful human beings as the model or paradigm of human forgiveness is a serious mistake. And yet it is a mistake baked into many Christians' understanding of forgiveness, and lies behind the lack of priority and attention given to what a harmer might do in order to facilitate moral repair, and restoration of what has been lost after harm. The Christian focus is almost invariably on what the harmed must do after harm. The harmer is rather quickly seen as irrelevant, and either ignored or tried and sent off to prison or otherwise excluded.

Almost every Christian post-harm practice and habit reinforces this dynamic, including the contemporary pastoral approach to interpersonal forgiveness that seems more at home in the therapist's consulting room or on a Buddhist retreat than at the heart of the Judaeo-Christian tradition. Unlike some of its trenchant critics – such as Gregory Jones, whose 1995 book *Embodying Forgiveness* mercilessly takes Lewis Smedes to task for his reductionism – I have no beef with those who see resentment as a mental health issue that needs priority attention. I'm also happy to include this within the gamut of a broad understanding of forgiveness, as I will explain later. But when we make such moves, we must remember that we are leaving the response and the responsibility of the harmer out of the equation. There can be good psychological or other contingent reasons for doing so, but maybe these should be exceptions. And we certainly need to lose all our coyness and hesitancy about the merits of repentance for human beings and institutions that are responsible for harm. This is a challenging message to communicate, made more difficult, it seems to me, by the increased enthusiasm for forgiveness in recent decades, which has coincided with the rise and rise of the therapeutic understanding of what forgiveness involves.

Release of resentful feelings towards those who have hurt you, or moving on from unforgiveness, is not something we read of in the Gospels. Indeed, it's hard to know where you might find it. One possibility that has occurred to me is in the parable of the Good Samaritan. If Jesus were focused on the importance of victims forgiving those who have harmed them, should the Good Samaritan not only have helped the man robbed and beaten by robbers to safety and paid for his accommodation and care costs, but also sat down with him and said, 'You can take or leave this, but I think you'll find you'll benefit if you resolve to forgive those guys'?

Please don't check to see where this exchange is in the Bible. It isn't. It couldn't be. The idea is a new one – as indeed are most of the thoughts we have today about interpersonal forgiveness. But even the recent monograph by David Konstan on the development of the modern concept of forgiveness[4] is not quite up to date, because he assumes most people's notion of forgiveness to mean the response by the victim to something like 'repentance' coming from the perpetrator.

The idea that the normative form of forgiveness is a psycho-spiritual project of releasing toxic emotions is something else. It certainly has its value, but so too does the notion that those who have harmed have options available to them which, while they might not make good the damage they have done, nonetheless have benefits. I shall discuss this further, but the three principal benefits I see flowing from serious repentance are, first, that both the harm and the responsibility for it are honestly recognized and acknowledged; secondly, that any attempt to make amends, in so far as is possible, will accrue some practical benefits for the *harmed*; and thirdly, that by doing such things a harmer might render themself more worthy of forgiveness, more forgivable.

I do not believe you can earn your forgiveness by repenting. After serious and life-changing harm even the most thorough and perfect repentance will leave a gap which can only be bridged from the forgiver's side. That forgiveness is a gift is fundamental, and an idea that can exist in perfect harmony with a sophisticated understanding of the nature and potential of repentance. Moreover, repentance, while it reduces the forgivability gap, does not remove the right of the victim to withhold forgiveness. This is because only a victim can appraise whether the repentance achieves a change in the harmer which convinces the harmed that it is safe, constructive and valuable for them to let go of whatever it is they hold against this particular harmer. To go back to Dryden, we might say that '*unforgiveness* to the injured doth belong.'

Does this mean that when we are hurt we acquire a 'victim-status' that means we are effectively judge and jury with regard to the person who has harmed us? I don't think so, because the 'moral powers of victims' don't extend that far. A decision not to forgive has no legal impact, and if it were to feature in a victim statement it should be seen for what it is – a statement about the victim's view of the perpetrator rather than a statement of the legal standing or actual guilt of the perpetrator, or even the objective nature of any repentance. That is not to say it should be dismissed, but it should be interpreted and weighed against other considerations.

The only sensible response to such thoughts is to recognize that *anything* can be weaponized. Forgiveness can be manipulated, victimhood can be exploited, repentance can be distorted into a mocking parody of itself if it is an emotive grandstanding about depths of sorrow or cheapened by a shoulder-shrugging 'all I can do is apologize.'

That repentance cannot earn forgiveness does not undermine the hugely important point that there are steps that can be taken to move the harmer in the direction of becoming more worthy of forgiveness. There are also post-harm actions a perpetrator or harmer might take that will make no difference whatsoever to their 'forgivability'. And there are others which make the person less forgivable by adding further insult to the already injured and insulted.

Repentance has a potentially huge and transformative role to play in addressing moral harm and facilitating relational repair after atrocious harms have been inflicted. Earlier we noticed how in Delia Owens' novel, *Where the Crawdads Sing*, Kya asks why, after harm, all the onus for forgiveness is placed on the injured, the still bleeding? This chapter has set out to explain this unreasonable and unjust state of affairs. It will not be properly addressed until repentance is given its due – and for that we need to understand its ethical and social nature, and potential corruptions, as well as its complex and convoluted theological history.

12

Repenting

If we want to draw on historical resources to develop our ideas about repentance, we need to turn to Judaism. While Christian theologians agonized for centuries about how the painful death of Jesus was necessary 'for the sins of the world', and in that respect a means of forgiveness, rabbis were working away at the question of what might meaningfully and effectively be done by those who realize they have sinned not against God, but against their neighbours. Among them is the twelfth-century Moses Ben Maimon, better known as Maimonides, who included extensive and practical 'Laws of Repentance' in the *Mishneh Torah*.

Rabbi Danya Ruttenberg has recently published an introduction to Maimonides' approach to repentance for a contemporary audience – Jews and Gentiles.[1] Maimonides was not concerned to be original in what he said, but collated and synthesized Jewish wisdom from all the available resources, filling gaps and adding his own reflections as would be appropriate for any living tradition. As Ruttenberg emphasizes, Maimonides sees repentance as a matter not just of making amends, but also of transformation. It's not done in a few words of apology, but involves a process or a set of steps. In this we can see Maimonides as the *über*-grandparent of the idea of putting a reparative process in place. In Judaism repentance is work – a word deeply problematic to Christians, who have sometimes seemed to think that even to suggest a person might do something to improve their behaviour is to undermine the free grace by which God forgives. But what is vital and interesting is the nature of this work. It is the work of *teshuva*, the work of returning. It's about getting back to where you were before you went wrong.

What are the steps? According to Ruttenberg they are:

1. Name and own the harm.
2. Starting to change.
3. Restitution and accepting consequences.
4. Apology.
5. Making different choices.

We could think of these steps of repentance as related to the 12-step programmes that are so important and effective in helping people manage their addictions. The object of engaging in such programmes, as I understand it, is healing from the results of former addictive behaviour and resilience to prevent further lapses. Repentance in Maimonides' sense is rather like this. It is not a means to forgiveness, but a way of sorting your own life out and integrating more of it around core and positive values. If you repent you become a better person. As a result, your chances of eliciting forgiveness from those you have harmed will have increased. You do not repent at the human level to be forgiven, but to put right. Repentance isn't the self-infliction of pain in order to appease a grumpy deity, or to offer payback through the coin of suffering to someone you have victimized.

It is moral spiritual self-improvement for the benefit of others, coupled with an effort to put things right, which makes repentance so vital, and which the Christian and psychological prioritizing of forgiveness can so easily distort. It can be wonderful when people forgive. However, like happiness, forgiveness is best approached not by turning it into a goal, aim or project, because that risks distorting it with narcissism, anxiety and hyper-cognition. Forgiveness is best served when those who have done wrong ask not, 'How can I be forgiven?' but rather, 'How far can I put things right?' How, in other words, can I engage with repentance from this particularly uncomfortable, distressed and blameworthy moment of my life? It is by aiming at repair, and considering only the needs of the harmed, that repentance can reduce the forgivability gap. But true repentance is not a self-interested pursuit. You do not repent for gain. You do it to change.

Maimonides' first step in repentance is to 'name and own the harm'. This is about acknowledging what has happened and taking responsibility. It is hard to imagine a situation in which acknowledgement of what one has done and what it has inflicted, and the acceptance that responsibility lies squarely on one's shoulder, would not be an appropriate first step for a perpetrator of serious harm. Otherwise, all subsequent steps would be nonsense. However, denial of the truth and defensiveness about the responsibility for harm (aggravated by fear of punishment) are extremely common. Acknowledgement and ownership are therefore a very serious step. Sometimes it might not be just one step, but a series of steps. Indeed, it might be that the full meaning of ownership, responsibility and acknowledgement only emerges later; that there are levels of acknowledgement and ownership. On the other hand, it might even be the case that this is the most difficult step and, if taken boldly, the rest might follow readily.

The second step is that the one who is repenting needs to begin to change. The reason I used a circumlocution in that sentence is that I think English-speakers really must make more use of that uncommon word. The noun that means 'one who repents' is 'penitent' – which takes us back to Jerome's choice of word in the fourth century and all that flowed from it. So the harmer who has acknowledged must start to change. The extent to which they do will depend on social factors such as the influences that have shaped their character and inform their life, and psychological ones such as their belief in their own capacities. But it matters hugely that the religious, in this case rabbinical, advice is: first own your responsibility, then start to change.

The third step presents further challenges, and to my mind contains within it two different ideas. 'Restitution' refers to returning what was removed as the harm was inflicted, and 'consequences' in particular to any penal or legal responses or other sanctions imposed by an authority. Accepting consequences is a fairly passive matter, but it is good that religion insists on it. The idea that repentance-forgiveness is a way of avoiding consequences is an old but persistent trick of unrepentant harmers. But we can be clear that in Maimonides' world, and indeed Ruttenberg's, we are not looking for a free pass here but a serious process of positive transformation.

Restitution is an interesting one. Christians are often unfamiliar and uncomfortable with this idea, seeing it perhaps as part of the whole dodgy business of earning your forgiveness. But from the same country as the TRC comes the slightly jokey but nonetheless serious notion of 'bicycle theology' – a shorthand for a situation where restitution is needed for forgiveness to make sense. This is my version of it.

> Jack steals Jill's bicycle. Jack feels bad about it and, having heard much about the power of forgiveness, gets the idea that this could provide the way out his predicament. So Jack goes to the bike-less Jill and apologizes, hoping to be forgiven. Being a South African, Jill has also heard about the power of forgiveness, and is aware that her irritation at being bike-less is affecting her happiness and how she relates to others. Jill really would like to forgive and put all this in the past. But then she has a thought. *If I forgive, what happens to the bicycle?*

Good question, Jill! The order of precedence here, as Maimonides makes clear, is first return the bicycle, and then apologize for having taken it. Then if you wish you may ask to be forgiven. However, to ask for forgiveness ahead of returning the bicycle – that really would be something else. What would we call it? 'Unforgivable!', perhaps. And we'd want to say to Jill, 'No, don't forgive him until he returns your bicycle.' And we'd assure her, I hope, that forgiveness-anxiety is not called for in such a situation.

But restitution isn't always possible. In the meantime, Jenny may have stolen the bike from Jack, in which case Jack might have to offer Jill something else, even if that is merely a deeper understanding of what it means to have your bicycle stolen. Restitution works well in terms of theft, but not every harm is a theft, even when it is analogous to one, as Susan Waters suggested regarding the abuse perpetrated by Bob C. But what Bob C. and other abusers have 'taken' – innocence and all that comes with it – could never be restored. The same is the case after murder, of course, and in many other contexts. Nevertheless, a sincere and well advised *repenter* will be positive about both restitution and reparations.

Maimonides' final step is the new thinking and behaviour of the person who has reformed since inflicting the harm. In this model the repentant person is not covered with shame and guilt for what they have done – they will have moved on from that, with or without forgiveness, and now be someone with better attitudes and better ethics making better decisions and, inevitably, a more purposeful and social contribution to the well-being of others and society.

Rabbi Ruttenberg claims that it's Judaism's emphasis on repentance rather than on forgiveness that makes it a more victim-centred and victim-friendly religion than Christianity. This is a startling claim – but is it fair? One question I asked myself as I read her book was, 'Would it be preferable to live in a society where, after harm had been inflicted, the primary cultural pressure was to do what could be done to help the harmer to repent, rather than help the harmed to forgive?' My answer was that I could see a lot of advantages in a society organizing itself around the challenge of promoting repentance and that, if I were creating a culture from scratch, I would make repentance a higher priority than forgiveness. On further reflection I wondered why I needed to think about it at all. Of course it's in everyone's interest if those who harm are encouraged to repent, and if necessary walked through the process. How might it be if social institutions, from religions to education establishments and prisons, had this on their agendas for human and community development – and indeed justice? It's not a familiar notion, but it needs airtime alongside protecting the public, delivering rehabilitation and restorative justice.

But repentance is a value as well as a practice, and has been elbowed out by punishment and forgiveness. It needs its space. And its place, I suggest, is above forgiveness. Concentrating on forgiveness and then, somewhat reluctantly, moving on to repentance, is the misapplication of the model of divine forgiveness, and in the human realm gets things the wrong way round. It also takes too narrow a view of the actual possibilities after someone has been harmed. Forgiveness and repentance, or repentance and forgiveness, shouldn't be considered ahead of the safety and well-being of the victim, say, or the punishment of the offender.

As I have mentioned, there are those who see punishment and forgiveness as alternatives, but I don't believe that's correct, except in the sense that amnesty, pardon and clemency are informally glossed as 'forgiveness'. But the dynamics and the consequences are quite different. Amnesty is freedom from sanction, forgiveness is release from being regarded in a certain way by your victims.

Repentance sits naturally in the conceptual and practical space between punishment and forgiveness.

It could take place alongside punishment, or instead of punishment if there was sufficient trust, or in cases where punishment is not appropriate. It is also something that can lead to or be prompted by forgiveness. Those who deliver restorative justice programmes are rightly wary of getting the idea tangled up with forgiveness, with good reason, as some intriguing research shows that forgiveness is more likely to occur in a restorative justice situation if it is not mentioned. The same could be the case with repentance. As a term with a religious history it might indeed be something it is not best to mention, but there is a clear overlap between repentance and restorative justice, in that both depend on the acknowledgement and ownership by the harmer, and both are predicated on the hope that there can be change. The difference, perhaps, is that restorative justice aims at the reform or education of the harmer, whereas repentance, in Maimonides' model, is victim-centred, as it makes a priority of putting things right for them. What this doesn't take into account is that for some victims a sense that the harmer is changing through the process of facing the consequences for others of their crimes, while not restitution, has satisfactions that can be reparative.

In the aftermath of harm, once judgements of guilt and responsibility have been made and the nature and extent of harm has been ascertained, I'd suggest there are five priorities for attention, best ordered as follows:

- The safety of the victim.
- The healing of the victim.
- The sanction of the perpetrator – whether that is rebuke or punishment or anything else that

restores the perpetrator to a position of dignity in society.
- The repentance of the perpetrator – that is, the perpetrator's attempt to make amends and become someone who would not repeat the offence, and thereby more 'forgivable'.
- The forgiveness of survivors – that is, the change of heart and mind that frees them from at least some of the indirect personal and relational consequences of the harm and restores goodwill.

It is only with an ordered view of these priorities that we can hope for a holistic and victim-friendly response to harm. In practical terms, the order in which they are addressed will vary, and they will overlap in complex ways. However, the point is not to theorize about the flow of a process but to identify the priorities of concern. If we put forgiveness on a pedestal, we lose this. If we neglect punishment, safety or healing, we also lose it. If we neglect repentance, we also lose it. And we also lose it if we think of any of these matters – safety, well-being, sanction, repentance and forgiveness – in simplistic or binary ways.

The first three priorities, the safety and health of the victim and the sanction of the perpetrator, are different in kind to repentance and forgiveness. They are necessary, but limited and constrained. Repentance and forgiveness are different in that they are grounded in hope, freedom and grace. And that is why they are of religious or spiritual significance in ways that safety, healing and sanction are not. They matter hugely and are vitally important for moral repair at the personal and social level, but they do not have the transformative potential of repentance and forgiveness.

My list of five is important after serious harm, but there are also occasions when repentance and forgiveness might be appropriate even though there aren't serious concerns about safety, well-being or sanction. And there might be cases where repentance is too heavy a word for what is appropriate from the harmer, the harm being so easily explained and temporary. Forgiveness may nonetheless be relevant and called for because bad feelings have arisen and one party holds something against the other, or feels there is a moral debt that needs to be addressed. This is another way of saying that the nature of forgiveness is contextual, something central to the argument of this book, and that grand, overarching theories of forgiveness, or indeed any imperatives regarding forgiveness, are likely to be unhelpful and misleading.

I have two huge issues with how repentance is currently understood. First, the place of remorse within repentance has been exaggerated to the extent that it has become a problem. We need to rethink remorse and downgrade it in relation to the more behavioural and cognitive aspects of repentance. Secondly, we need to recognize that apology is a complex and potentially problematic matter. As with remorse, therefore, even if a victim-friendly approach to the aftermath of harm will prioritize repentance, that repentance will be of a subtle and not very emotional kind. This is not to say that the repentance I'm arguing for becomes a dry, heartless or formulaic matter; on the contrary: I have a holistic understanding of repentance. Making more space for changes of behaviour and thought within my understanding of repentance inevitably leaves less for emotional responses to having harmed. But there is another consideration here, which is that repentance that is focused on emotional change and expression is more ambiguous and more inclined to add to the pressures on the victim – something which a harmer whose repentance is disingenuous will know and exploit. Remorse-light repentance is much less prone to manipulation.

What I hope to persuade you is that the worse the harm, the less relevant remorse-filled apology will be. Above all, I want to suggest that remorse-filled apology after abuse, exploitation, oppression and the like is irrelevant to the harmed, indeed an imposition on them that they are fully entitled to consider as further harm.

If that sounds negative, let's take the positive step of identifying what the characteristics of a healthy and victim-friendly apology might be. I can think of six. A good apology is one in which the harmer acknowledges that they are responsible for inflicting harm, and communicates that in a suitably modest and respectful, but not overly emotional, way. This is the most important message of all, and reflects the first stage in Maimonides' understanding of repentance. The other messages the apologizer needs to convey are that they:

- feel they now understand both the wrongfulness of their actions and that the harm inflicted was extensive – but not fully knowable to anyone other than the harmed;
- would like to be able to put matters right, but appreciate that the only way to do that would be to put the clock back, something they long to do but know they cannot;

- wish it to be known that if there is anything they can do to alleviate any of the burden inflicted by the harm, they will make a serious effort to provide it;
- are grateful for the time and attention the harmed person has given in attending to the apology, and hope it has not caused them any further harm;
- want the harmed to know that they have learned from reflecting on the harm inflicted, and believe they are no longer the person who would inflict such harm.

This is admittedly quite a long list. However, to some it might be more remarkable for what it omits. Three omissions are noteworthy. The absence of the word 'sorry'. The absence of any expression of remorse. The absence of any request for forgiveness. In the next chapter we will explore each of these in turn.

13

Sorry

Mina Smallman is a retired senior Church of England minister; in fact, she was the first black woman to rise to the rank of archdeacon. In 2019 two of her daughters, Bibaa Henry and Nicole Smallman, were enjoying an evening together in a park in London. They were outside because of Covid restrictions. However, the night ended in tragedy when they were both murdered by Danyal Hussein, a 19-year-old satanist. Unbelievably, two of the police officers at the crime scene posed with the mutilated corpses for selfies, which they then shared with colleagues on WhatsApp groups in which the murdered women were referred to as 'dead birds'. One group, which consisted of no fewer than 41 police officers, was called 'the A team', and the other, of friends of one of the officers, was called 'Covid cunts'.

Later the Metropolitan Police issued a statement apologizing for 'falling short' and compounding the 'distress felt by their loved ones'. If this was intended to placate the bereaved mother it failed. 'Say sorry?' she fumed in an interview in the *Guardian*. 'You know sorry is what you say when you bump into someone in the street.'[1]

Sorry, they say, is the hardest word, but it can also be a weak and trivializing one, an easy and inappropriate word – and especially if it is coupled with the word 'if'. 'I am sorry if . . .' is never going to work as an apology in a situation where serious harm has been inflicted. Still less if there is reference to having 'caused any upset' or similar. The word 'sorry' is a minefield for givers and receivers of apologies, as it detracts from the most important aspects of the message. Clarity about responsibility, intention to reform, offers of restitution and attempts to repair will always be undermined by equivocation. But they are also obscured by trying to find the words to convey the emotion of remorse, profundity of contrition or depth of sorrow. It can sometimes be better to say nothing.

It should not be thought that Mina Smallman is an unforgiving person. As Simon Hattenstone wrote in his *Guardian* feature,

> Throughout it all, she showed an astonishing dignity and capacity for forgiveness. She forgave the killer because he was obviously sick. And when the two officers were eventually sentenced, last December, to 33 months in jail after pleading guilty to misconduct in public office, she said she was prepared to meet them as part of a restorative justice process.

However, that forgiving spirit has evaporated as far as the police officers and the Met are concerned. Mina rescinded her willingness to meet the officers when they appealed against their conviction, as she did not want it to be used by them. Her views regarding the killer are different, however. 'Mina finds it difficult to forgive the government hypocrisy or the police officers,' writes Hattenstone,

> but none of her anger is directed at the killer. She pities him. She mentions Gee Walker, the mother of Anthony Walker, who was brutally murdered in an unprovoked racist attack 17 years ago. After his murder, '[Gee] said, "I forgive the killers because my faith tells me I should." I *preached* on that, saying, this woman is amazing because I'm not sure I could do it.'
>
> And has she done? She pauses. 'Yeah, I've forgiven Hussein.' Would she meet him? 'No, because he clearly isn't well. Maybe with some therapy support, years later that might be possible.'

Hattenstone also asks Mina if she has any advice for other people looking to forgive.

> I would say to someone who has lost their child in extreme circumstances, try to let the anger go. You're not letting your loved one down by letting go. If you imagine them looking down, they would be so upset that you have punctuated your life so the aggressor, the murderer, wins. Let the anger go.

That Mina Smallman distinguishes so clearly between her forgiveness of the murderer and her non-forgiveness of the police officers and the Met makes her example especially powerful, as does the fact that the person who has been forgiven has not apologized.

Saying sorry is, I suggest, a not very adept way of expressing remorse. But my message here isn't, 'Find a better way of expressing remorse,'; rather, 'Think about keeping it to yourself.' I appreciate that I'm rowing against the tide here. Shakespeare was convinced of the power of expressed remorse. For instance, in *The Two Gentlemen of Verona* it seems remorse is considered to be a straightforward, convincing and effective method of soliciting forgiveness. Proteus repeatedly deceives Valentine and attempts to rape Silvia, but then makes a speech.

> My shame and my guilt confounds me.
> Forgive me, Valentine: if hearty sorry
> Be a sufficient ransom for offence,
> I tender't here, I do as truly suffer,
> As e'er I did commit.

Valentine accepts this:

> Then I am paid;
> And once again I do receive thee honest . . .
> Who by repentance is not satisfied
> Is nor of heaven nor earth, for these are pleased.
> By penitence the Eternal's wrath's appeased.

We note that the remorse-laden request for forgiveness bypasses the intended rape victim. That is, I think, inevitable with this sort of transactional approach whereby a 'victim' can consider himself paid, appeased or satisfied by the expression of shame and guilt. Note too that Valentine in his short acceptance speech references divine forgiveness and connects the costliness of shame and guilt with penitence. I refer to this not because I think people today get their ethics by reading Shakespeare but because it draws attention to how deeply embedded in our literary culture is the myth that remorse is a kind of magic that resolves human relationships after harm. Had Valentine said, 'Don't be so ridiculously self-pitying. Your remorse means nothing to me. Go cry in your beer!' theatre-goers down the centuries would have absorbed a very different message.

Real victims, on the other hand, are not looking for words like 'sorry' or expressions of remorse. Nor are they seeking retribution. In Ariel Dorfman's play *Death and the Maiden* – now also a Hollywood movie, set in a post-junta South American country, a woman named Paula finds herself face-to-face with the man who tortured her. She has managed to get him tied to a chair and has him under her control – can do what she wishes with him. But what does she actually *want*?

> I want him to confess. I want him to sit down in front of that cassette recorder and tell me what he did – not just to me, everything, to everybody – and then have him write it out in his own handwriting and sign it and I would keep a copy forever – with all the information, the names and data, all the details. That's what I want.[2]

She just needs acknowledgement.

An example from a real-life atrocity adds another layer to the argument.

Michael Lapsley is an Anglican priest who as a young New Zealander went to South Africa and became a monk. His experiences of life quickly persuaded him that he had to become an active anti-apartheid campaigner. Just before the end of the apartheid era he was sent a letter bomb that he opened at his breakfast. It blew off his hands, destroyed one eye and burst his eardrums. In his memoir *Redeeming the Past* he addresses the subject of forgiveness, but the book is not the story about how he came to forgive the person who made and sent the letter bomb. Lapsley's distinctions in this area are subtle and important. He is chronically disabled by his injuries, but says he is not overwhelmed by the 'unforgiving emotions'. In his view, perpetrators must take responsibility for their actions if there is to be what he calls 'full reconciliation'.

> In my case the bomb that almost killed me was not dropped from the sky in an impersonal act of war. My name, Fr Michael Lapsley, was carefully inscribed on the envelope. It was a chilling act that links me forever with the unknown person who wrote it. Since I am not full of hatred and bitterness and my heart has softened, forgiveness is potentially on the table. For me, forgiveness is an I-thou process, and since I don't know who bombed me, there is as yet no one to forgive. If someone were to come forward and say, 'I am the person who sent you the bomb. Please forgive me,' I would be willing to turn the key that frees that person from guilt. But first I would need to know if he still makes letter bombs. I live in Cape Town around the corner from the largest children's hospital in Africa, and if the person said, 'Ah, I work at that hospital,' I would know that he had had a change of heart. My response would be, 'Yes of course, I forgive you.' How much better that my assailant should continue working in a hospital rather than being locked up in prison. This is the justice of restoration,

> not the justice of punishment. But there is more. In my imagination I might then sit down for a cup of tea with the bomber, now my friend, and during the conversation I might say, 'You know, even though I've forgiven you, I still have no hands; I still have only one eye; and I still hear very poorly. Of course, there is nothing you can do to bring these things back, but because of what you did I will need assistance for the rest of my life. Of course you will help to pay for that.' In this case my forgiveness is not conditional on restitution, but restitution is necessary to heal fully the relationship between the two of us.[3]

This is an important passage for anyone interested in what forgiveness might involve today. Although close to Desmond Tutu in many ways, Lapsley's model of forgiveness here is not the Tutu model we have already encountered. He distances himself from the forgiveness-is-good-for-you approach. He has not forgiven, but he is not burdened by unforgiveness. In his words, his heart has softened. Like Gordon Wilson of Enniskillen, he seems to have no ill-will. But unlike Gordon Wilson he knew that his name was literally on the bomb that almost killed him; it was 'carefully inscribed on the envelope' – and so he feels bonded with the bomber. It is this very bonding that creates the gap which might be addressed by forgiveness or reconciliation. Yet that cannot happen without responsibility, in his words, echoing Maimonides and Ruttenberg.

Lapsley mentions neither apology nor remorse. He is interested in what the bomber is doing, not how he feels. This is perhaps because his emotions have moved on. But he insists on restitution. For him this would come after an act of forgiveness, something from him that would 'turn the key that frees that person from guilt'. For him, then, forgiveness is by no means the end of the story; rather it is a new beginning that leads to the possibility of further healing and more justice.

It is also significant that Lapsley imagines sitting down and chatting with the bomber. He has told us some of what he would want to discuss in that conversation, but now he has created the scenario I want him to ask more questions of the bomber. So let me add mine.

> *Tell me, were you a lone ranger or part of a team? Was the bomb your idea or were you acting on orders? Was this a one-off for you, or did you make or send more – is there more blood than mine on your hands? And now we are talking, what can you tell me about your life before you sent the bomb? Were you a violent person in your relationships, or is bombing the only outlet for your hostility and aggression? And how about the influences on you in your younger days? Did you have a good and positive upbringing, or were you deprived, even abused, and given poor role models? And what about hatred? I experienced the bomb very, very personally. Was it personal for you, or was I just an abstract enemy?*

Perhaps my curiosity is running away with me, but as I enter into the situation with as much empathy as I can muster, I want to know more and more about this bomber. But I remain decidedly uninterested in whether the bomber feels remorse, is inclined to apologize or is about to come out with 'Sorry'. Should the bomber be identified, either through detective work or coming forward to confess, the truth is he will have a whole complex of feelings, and the consequences he faces will inevitably see his remorse caught up in self-pity. One of the problems with remorse is that it is so hard to distinguish from ordinary, narcissistic regret. But the more it is pushed forward, the more suspect it seems.

Time, a 2021 BBC TV drama series written by Jimmy McGovern, explores the experiences in prison of Mark Cobden, a schoolteacher who had killed a pedestrian while driving his car over the limit for alcohol. Cobden is full of remorse, guilt and shame, and wants to write to the dead man's widow. He agonizes before putting some words on paper, but does send a letter. Ultimately it is rejected by the widow and returned to him, but an experienced prison warder who looks at it comments, 'I have seen a lot of these, and this is about the best.' The letter consists of just one word repeated over and over again. 'SORRY'.

This brief but brilliant yet dark moment from a brilliant but dark series sums up the problem with the word 'sorry'. It is both the only word that is appropriate and, in cases of serious harm, entirely inappropriate. As are many expressions of regret, remorse or apology. Should you confess your sins to a priest in the hope of divine absolution it absolutely matters that you do so in a spirit of contrition. It is, after all, a spiritual exercise for your benefit. However, to seek to 'repent' of wrongdoing that has harmed another person is a different kind of activity with ethical and relational aspects. The aim here should not be to do what it necessary for you to be forgiven, but to make some kind of contribution, however inadequate, to the repair and restoration of the one you have wronged and harmed. Repentance before your harmed neighbour is a very different matter to repenting before your sinned-against God.

In Henry Fielding's novel *Tom Jones*, Tom wants to marry Sophia Western, but things get very difficult when she becomes aware of his sexual escapades. Feeling he is beyond all hope of forgiveness, he expresses remorse. 'No repentance was ever more sincere. O! let it reconcile me to my heaven in this dear bosom'. To me the reference to heaven suggests he is hoping to leverage the Christian value of forgiveness, but the aptly named Sophia puts her finger on the difference between divine and human responses to contrition.

> 'Sincere repentance, Mr Jones', answered she, 'will obtain the pardon of a sinner, but it is from one who is the perfect judge of that sincerity. A human mind may be imposed on; nor is there any infallible method to prevent it. You must expect, however, that if I can be prevailed upon by your repentance to pardon you, I will at least insist on the strongest proof of sincerity.'[4]

Tom gladly accepts the challenge, but when he invites her to state her criterion, he receives an answer he did not want: 'Time'.

The problem with the idea that remorse matters to the harmed is shown very clearly in this eighteenth-century novel. There are various ways you could express it. Philosophically, expressions of remorse raise the problem of other minds – you can never be sure you really know what someone else is thinking or feeling. In terms of personal integrity, we might question the extent to which the remorseful one is self-aware or self-deceiving.

Is all that emotion for me, the recipient may wonder, or is it the narcissistic wound that is causing the pain and the apology a way of dealing with that? And remember, we are talking about a report of an emotional state. A protestation of deep sorrow may be sincere, but does it reflect any change in the traits of character, the values held and the habits acquired that lay behind the harmful behaviour? The suspicious recipient of a remorse-laden apology may suspect that not much has changed under the top dressing of tears. Or we might also look at this in terms of power dynamics.

The sort of interpersonal remorse we are thinking of here is not that of a student who turns in an assignment late, or a child who has annoyed their parents by failing to tidy up a mess. The most serious challenges for forgiveness always come in situations where power has been abused and trust betrayed. And in the aftermath of such injuries, expressions of feeling are far too easy, far too epistemologically dubious, and far too potentially manipulative to be considered relevant.

And in any case, what I've suggested constitutes an adequate apology leaves the penitent harmer with plenty to do other than emote.

Lastly, what can we say about asking for forgiveness? Is it precisely what the repentant harmer should do, or is it something they should never do? Opinions differ sharply. The former Protestant terrorist Alistair Little is very clear. 'As a perpetrator, I would never ask the forgiveness of the family of a man I shot dead. They have suffered enough without having to respond to that kind of request from me.'[5] I remember when I first read this stopping to think the point through. As a Christian who engages in traditional liturgy, I am asking for forgiveness all the time. Consider the prayers that constitute the 'ordinary' of the mass, which has been the backbone of Catholic worship for centuries. These prayers, mostly known by their Latin names, have been set to music countless times. They are the *Kyrie eleison* – a prayer for God's mercy; the *Gloria in excelsis deo* – which includes prayers for mercy; the *Credo* which includes a statement of belief in one baptism for the forgiveness of sins; and the *Agnus dei*, in which the Lamb of God who takes away the sins of the world is approached twice with the petition to 'have mercy upon us'. This repetition doesn't exhaust the list of forgiveness prayers in the mass, for we also have the confession of sins which ensures that the penitential thrust of the occasion isn't lost in the music of Giovanni Palestrina or William Byrd.

However, I do think Little is right. Asking for forgiveness of God is one thing. Asking it of someone we have seriously harmed can have all the faults of remorse-laden apology – and then some.

The philosopher Myisha Cherry (no relation), Associate Professor at the University of California, Riverside, has given extended consideration to the different ways in which people might go about asking for forgiveness in her book *The Failures of Forgiveness*. She lists seven different approaches, including commands, pleas, invitations and apologies. I am more inclined to warm to those that clearly make space for the harmed person to come to a response in their own time and without any sort of pressure.

One example she gives invites us deeper into this question of how this matter is best approached. It comes from the 1995 movie adaptation of Sister Helen Prejean's book *Dead Man Walking*. Directed and co-produced by Tim Robbins, it stars Susan Sarandon as Prejean, a nun who becomes spiritual adviser to Mark Poncelet, a prisoner on death row for the rape and murder of a teenage couple. Cherry alights upon the moment just before Poncelet is administered the lethal injection that will end his life, when he speaks to some of those gathered to witness his execution. 'Mr Delacroix,' he says to the father of one of his victims, 'I don't want to leave this world with any hate in my heart. I ask your forgiveness for what I done. It was a terrible thing I done in taking our son away from you.'

Myisha Cherry praises this because it satisfies three particular conditions: 'He confesses to the crime, shows remorse, and acknowledges the pain he has inflicted.'[6] I agree that there is remorse here, but it is subtle and decidedly not the main event. The key phrase is the almost unadorned, 'it is a terrible thing I done.' This acknowledgement and realism in the harmer are far more significant and helpful than any expression of emotion. Also significant is that Poncelet does not wait for a response but goes on to speak to other family members. That could be for many reasons, but it would have been a very different matter had he put any pressure on Delacroix to answer.

Such an approach seems to me very different from Karl's to Simon Wiesenthal, and had Poncelet made the sort of move the SS officer made on 'a Jew' I would feel very differently. But he sought no consolation, and his words, whether they were helpful or not, were respectful of the harmed. That's the litmus.

Having reflected on Myisha Cherry's analysis of the various ways of asking for forgiveness, I feel what might have been labelled the *optative* approach is by far the best. The lack of presumption and pressure in saying, 'I hope you can forgive me,' is attractive; unless the person who says it is being cruelly arch or ironic then it is likely to be a statement that comes out of a genuine repentance. A gentle expression of hope lacks the impossible pomposity of a command to forgive, or the cloying and manipulative requests that can so easily elide into commands: can you, will you, will you please, oh, come on, for goodness' sake forgive. Or, as Nina Raine's play *Consent* ends, 'Forgive me. Fucking forgive me.'

I've spent much of this chapter being negative about saying sorry, expressing remorse and asking for forgiveness. But don't conclude that apology is an inevitably corrupt practice. A good apology, perhaps followed by a gentle expression of the hope that forgiveness might one day be possible, can be honouring, dignifying, honest and helpful. On the other hand, apologies that are laden with emotion or not thought through, or which reveal nothing more than that the harmer finds themself in an ethical, spiritual and verbal *cul-de-sac* – like Mark Cobden's letter to the woman he bereaved – are unhelpful or worse in the aftermath of serious harm.

14

Forgiving

What is forgiveness? The truth, I believe, is that there is not one straightforwardly definable form of forgiveness but that a variety of responses to having been harmed might count as forgiveness. In the hope that it will provide a useful map of the forgiveness territory I will consider three different but related kinds of forgiveness: private, gift and responsive.

Private forgiveness is forgiveness as a subtle but deep and sometimes dynamic and transformative change that takes place entirely within the forgiver. Others may help or guide them towards forgiveness, but this is not integral to the process. You could do this sort of forgiving entirely on your own and no one else need ever know. The following are the most familiar examples:

- Forswearing or dropping resentment, anger, rage or indignation.
- Overcoming feelings of vengefulness and either not taking revenge or desisting from taking revenge.
- Releasing ill-will towards the harmer.
- Eliminating as far as possible the harming action and its insult from one's mind.

- Writing off any moral debt that is understood to exist.
- Letting go of anything held against the harmer.

For many people today private forgiveness, involving all or some of the above, is now the primary way of thinking about forgiveness. But can there be aspects to private forgiveness that are not about releasing or letting go? First, 'Restoring or developing goodwill' towards the harmer would be a step further than 'releasing ill-will', but it need not lead to the step of reconnecting or reconciling. Another might be, 'Deciding not to hate or to let bitterness take root'. This is a proactive and personal decision and, while it might be entirely private, some who focus on this aspect of forgiving also see the wider implications and make it public, as we shall discuss later. A third form might be, 'Moving on from feelings of guilt or shame that arose as a result of having been harmed'. Plainly understood, guilt and shame belong to the harmer, not the harmed, and yet in many cases of serious abuse and exploitation the harmed themselves carry a burden of guilt – and it often takes them months, if not years or decades, to understand that these are not the most appropriate feelings. However, there can also be ambiguities about responsibility, and when the harmed one might be right to feel guilt and shame. I say this not to encourage victim-blaming, but to introduce self-forgiveness.

Self-forgiveness is now a popular and important idea, but has been seen by those who have a clear ethical or theological definition of forgiveness as problematic. The problem being, to use a technical term, that the self has no *standing* to forgive the self. Against this are put various arguments which in essence propose that there are different forms of self-forgiveness. Among them is the idea that to forgive the self is not to self-absolve, but to intentionally manage down the psychological aspects of self-blame so that life becomes bearable. There is also the idea that we rightly forgive ourselves when we feel we have let ourselves down by our actions, or on occasions when we are both the harmed and the harmer. Another strong argument is that the human self is not a simple integral unity but is intrinsically multiple and diverse. On this understanding every sub-person or facet of our personality is in relationship with every other sub-person or facet, and sometimes it is necessary for one to be forgiving towards the other if we are not to pull ourselves apart.

I was a slow convert to the idea that self-forgiveness might be meaningful, my concern being that self-forgiveness might be used when repentance is more appropriate. To those who remain dubious about it I would suggest that if it is reasonable to talk about self-judgement and self-harm then it is also acceptable to talk about self-forgiveness. What matters is that we recognize that there are limits to the psychological and ethical possibilities of self-forgiving, and don't allow ourselves to think that forgiving ourselves makes any difference to those we have harmed or impacts on their sense of our guilt.

The other aspect of private forgiveness might be called 'Absorbing the cost'. It is often suggested that to forgive is costly, and the idea here seems to be a working through of the intuition that being harmed is like theft; it robs us of something. Susan Waters made this point about the impact of abuser Bob C. not only on her and her brother but also on her household. This connects, of course, with the idea that forgiveness involves writing off a moral debt. But absorbing the cost feels different from writing off the debt. (I appreciate that the metaphors – absorption, theft, cost, debt – are piling up here.)

What happens in private forgiveness is deep and mysterious, and we need to be varied and flexible in our use of language to do these ineffable matters justice. My inclination would be to keep going with the metaphors: to think of forgiveness as depending on an inner filtration process, whereby the harmed person takes control over the porosity of the filter. Or, to move the absorption idea away from the cost model, to think in terms of digestion preceding absorption. First we digest the harm we have experienced, analyse it, break it down into its basic components, noting its causes and impacts, and thereby come to a more fine-grained understanding of what happened and why. Then we move on to the next stage, which might be to absorb some of it, and finally we void what remains – voiding being another form of 'release'. What I find helpful about this slightly yukky metaphor is that it recognizes that, much as release from the impact of harm may be desirable, it is unlikely ever to be complete or total when the harm has been traumatic or life-changing. Some of it you have to live with, retain, remember – but not all.

Private forgiveness achieves the end of peace of mind by removing the various causes and aspects of inner disquiet that those who are harmed suffer. The forgiven, of course knows nothing about it, and the risks to the forgiver are minimal. But are there any hidden risks with private forgiveness, if one moves beyond the individual and considers the wider context?

Let me put it this way. If the feelings and thoughts that are generated by being harmed are dealt with entirely privately they will not make any difference in the real world. At the micro level this might not matter. But this is where considerations of power, oppression and exploitation become so important. If people get too proficient at forgiving, no one will ever get angry enough to demand justice for, say, rape victims, or abused children, or those who suffer from racism, sexism, ageism and so on.

This is not a new point, of course. The young Jane Eyre made it to her acquiescent and self-consciously forgiving friend Helen. But just as forgiveness has gained a new kudos in recent years, so have some found it necessary to speak out against the ethical and political danger of the world becoming too forgiving. What is sometimes called 'cancel culture' is perhaps symptomatic of this. So too is the increased use of the word 'unforgivable' as an expression of moral opprobrium or ethical disgust. These are both attempts to mitigate any watering down of accountability or eroding of ethical standards that a pro-forgiveness approach might encourage.

Those who are ardent enthusiasts for private forgiveness on the other hand might ask themselves whether drug-induced or surgically achieved removal of negative emotions, hostile thoughts and the desire for revenge, can be thought of as forgiveness. Forgiveness is too messy and predictable to be thought of as a decision and probably cannot be achieved at will, but it does need to involve some intentionality on the part of the forgiver, even if they feel their agency is limited.

Gift forgiveness by contrast, focuses not on what is going on inside a person, but on what they offer or present to the one they are forgiving; it is something shared, not hidden. It may be verbal or behavioural: the words 'I forgive you' may or may not be spoken. Gift forgiveness can precede private forgiveness or follow it. Psychologists distinguish between emotional and decisional forgiveness, and this is a related but different distinction to the one I am making here. In my understanding private forgiveness may not be more than a matter of emotional change, and gift forgiveness involves more than making a decision to forgive – it involves some sort of communication, some sort of delivery. What gift forgiveness has in common with decisional forgiveness is that the gift may be given at a relatively early stage in the inner-change process. We may, for instance, forgive someone in a tentative way – knowing that if it doesn't go well we will soon be back in unforgiveness territory. Some have referred to this as 'invitatory forgiveness': forgiveness given in the hope that it will precipitate repentance or otherwise lead to the freeing up of a relationship that has become blocked. Alternatively, gift forgiveness might take the form of a promise, vow or commitment. This is Professor Kathryn Norlock's understanding of what lies at the heart of forgiveness. It is not saying, 'I no longer hold this against you' or 'I have dropped all my anger and resentment and never have any vengeful thoughts when your duplicitous and hurtful actions return to my mind.' It means, 'I intend to do all I can *not* to hold this against you, but am not there yet.' I suspect at least some examples of gift forgiveness that get reported publicly have this quality of a vow or commitment rather than achievement. They are promises rather than reports.

There are a number of different ways of thinking about what is given in gift forgiveness. These might include:

- Re-establishing contact with the harmer.
- Restoring goodwill towards the harmer.
- Assuring the harmer that, as far as you are concerned, it's over – the moral debt has been wiped off, any cost has been absorbed.
- Reporting to the harmer that the inner work of private forgiveness is effectively complete, perhaps by saying, 'I have forgiven you.'
- Forgiving in a literal and performative way – i.e. actually saying, 'I forgive you'.
- Allowing the harmer to respond to the gift perhaps by saying, 'I accept your forgiveness.'
- Saying whatever else might need to be said to release the harmer from recrimination, guilt and shame.

In short, gift forgiveness may be based on some or all of the practices of private forgiveness, but adds to it an act of communication and a number of possible positive practices.

There are many risks with gift forgiveness. The gift may not be accepted, or it might be actively rejected or even resented, and seen as an accusation. Or it may be experienced, by the harmer or by observers, as patronizing or unnecessary. If the harmer denies that they are responsible or feels the harmed person is exaggerating the impact of the harm, then gift forgiveness is more likely to inflame than settle matters. Another danger with gift forgiveness, especially if it comes from a close third party, or in a situation where there are multiple primary victims, is that it may be misunderstood as a gift made on behalf of all – or as a comprehensively absolving or pardoning form of forgiveness.

In the case of gift forgiveness the end might be relief from the pressure to forgive, or the feeling that forgiveness is a duty, or the satisfaction that a very admirable free choice has been made. Can gift forgiveness be abused? Yes. I once heard a story of an elderly woman who, knowing she was close to death, summoned several people to her bedside so that she could forgive each of them for offences or injuries she still resented, whether or not they had any recollection of them at all.

These are, I think, necessary and unavoidable risks. They can be mitigated by careful use of words but, given the mess and muddle that attaches to questions of forgiveness in today's culture, misunderstandings are inevitable. The harmed need courage if they are to forgive as well as generosity of spirit and hope – the hope that words, feelings, attitudes can make a difference, and that there is an alternative to retribution, vengefulness and hatred. Gift forgiveness also requires a sense of timing and some sort of supporting narrative or commentary. In the case of Figen Murray this was provided by her interpretation of the two photographs – the one reminding her that the bomber was once an innocent, and the other touching her heart as an example of the selfless protection of a hostile enemy. In the case of Gordon Wilson in Enniskillen the narrative was the context of the Troubles, and the need that so many felt for a response to violence that was not itself violent. None of these narratives are strong enough to cause forgiveness, but they are enough to help narrow the forgivability gap; to make it clear that forgiveness is more than a grand emotional gesture. It is when gift forgiveness has integrity and depth, and when it fits the moment, that it has both meaning and impact.

This sort of gift forgiveness after serious harm can also have an agenda. This could be described as an attempt to 'change the narrative', to make a public and therefore political statement that not only affirms your own non-retaliatory, un-hateful un-resenting stance but also promotes this as a superior approach. 'I forgive. I will not retaliate. I will not hate. I am taking a stance against this sort of behaviour. There is another way.'

It is not uncommon for those who forgive publicly to draw attention to the fact that they are avoiding the path of hatred. For instance, Gee Walker of Liverpool, who publicly forgave those who had been arrested for the racist murder of her son Anthony in 2005, said,

> I can't hate. We're a forgiving family and it extended to outside, so it wasn't hard to forgive because we don't just preach it, we practise it.
>
> I brought up my children in this church to love. I teach them to love, to respect themselves, and respect others.
>
> What does bitterness do? It eats you up inside, it's like a cancer. We don't want to serve a life sentence with those people.[1]

In this regard gift forgiveness can be powerful and strong – though, as in the case of Gordon Wilson, it might be most effective if expressed gently and indirectly. Such gift forgiveness is an attempt to light a candle at a time of deep and potentially overwhelming bleakness. A genuine gift may or may not bring peace of mind or relieve a burden – and of course for some it is a way of walking deeper into controversy.

Does it make sense to offer gift forgiveness when you don't know who is responsible for your harm? Michael Lapsley, whose hands were blown off by a parcel bomb, clearly thinks not. His heart has softened, he has no hatred, he isn't going to be vengeful, but he sees the threshold for forgiving on the far side of an important conversation with the person who made and sent the bomb that exploded in his hands – something that comes out of an I-thou encounter, as he put it. No encounter, no gift, one might say.

Others may find themselves challenged when they subsequently learn more about the harmer and their motives. The South African TRC worked with the theory that knowing the truth facilitates reconciliation. That is sometimes true, but if you discover that the person who harmed you denies responsibility, or seeks to have their punishment reduced, or lets it be known that they continue to hate you and have no remorse whatsoever – then maybe that's the moment when the gift needs to be taken back. The deeper truth here might be that a gift cannot be given unless it is received.

Given all this, one can see the attractions of private forgiveness. Gift forgiveness has the great ethical and civil advantage of speaking into the public square in the aftermath of terrible harm. People such as Gordon Wilson, Gee Walker and Figen Murray deserve the recognition they receive, and should be supported by society at large when they are singled out for hostility and criticism by those who cannot identify with their forgiving attitude.

The third type of forgiveness I'll designate as 'responsive'. What differentiates responsive forgiveness from gift forgiveness is that in responsive forgiveness it is not the one who has been harmed who makes the first move, but the harmer. Responsive forgiveness is far more sophisticated than it might appear. The playground model of forgiveness – harm leads to upset which, if met by apology, elicits forgiveness – is of course 'responsive' and it is extraordinarily persistent. Yet it is inadequate as a way of understanding how things might helpfully and restoratively develop after *serious* harm.

In talking about responsive forgiveness I am deliberately avoiding the use of words such as repentance, remorse or apology, or invoking the notion of 'conditionality'. These words are problematic when used to describe 'that which is required from the harmer by the harmed before they will forgive'. The needs of the victim or survivor must be paramount, and any ethical or religious reservations about the rightness of any act of forgiveness must be articulated carefully and with respect. It is not appropriate for those who theorize about forgiveness or seek to promote it religiously to pronounce in terms of generalizations, for instance that it is imperative to forgive 'unconditionally', or that only forgiveness that follows repentance is ethical and good. Equally, the harmed person will be wise if they monitor their own vulnerability. Recovery after harm can be precarious, and could be jeopardized by engaging with the harmer. There might be occasions when it is best not to risk recovery by trying to get a clear sense of what the harmer now means or intends.

Any or all of the negative and positive practices of private and gift forgiveness might be involved in the drama of responsive forgiving, but the list needs to be extended to include various things the harmed need to do while they work out how best to respond to whatever the harmer presents. So I would add:

- Evaluating the harmer's words and attitude – is it genuine, authentic, appropriate, honest, realistic, or just another power-play?
- Forming a view of the nature and quality of any repenting, and where the harmer might be with regard to not only acknowledgement but also restitution (where's the bicycle now?).
- Accepting, or not, any apology.
- Accepting, or not, any request for forgiveness.
- Agreeing to participate in mediation or a restorative justice process.
- Supporting or advocating for a reduction in penalty or punishment for the harmer.

In cases where the damage done is relatively slight, or where it can be repaired, the harmer, and indeed connected observers, are entitled to have a view about whether or not any repentance is adequate, and the harmed could find themselves in the wrong if they are not proportionate in giving and withholding forgiveness. However, after traumatic harm or in cases where things cannot be put right, the harmed have a kind of sovereignty with regard to how they respond, and it is not for anyone other than the harmed themselves to make a judgement about whether any repentance, action or attitude, is adequate. Serious harm creates an unpayable moral debt, a 'forgivability gap' which can never be bridged from the harmer's side. Forgiveness in such situations can never be earned. It's not that all traumatic harm is unforgivable but forgiveness flows from freedom and there are situations in which no repentance can put a duty on the harmed. Forgiveness flows from freedom as well as from courage and generosity of spirit and can never be coerced. It is never justified or earned; after serious harm it is always given across a forgivability gap.

Responsive forgiveness is vulnerable to various risks. Depending on the nature of the harm and the relationship within which it took place, to be approached by someone who has harmed you could be worrying, or worse. Is the approach genuine, or manipulative? Does the person want to put things right or to take something more away – that nice feeling of having been forgiven? There are further possible responses still. Sometimes it might be right to respond like Simon Wiesenthal with silence. In another situation we might feel that an approach is burdensome and unhelpful and want to say, 'No, I'm not ready for this.' Manifestly disrespectful or impudent requests might get very short shrift.

If the approach from the harmer seems to constitute a demand to be forgiven then the situation is potentially very difficult indeed, especially if the harmed person is inclined to forgive and sees forgiveness as a good thing in itself – the more so if they have already achieved private forgiveness or were on the cusp of offering gift forgiveness. Now the minimizing or demanding response has only inflicted further harm – and insult. Under such circumstances the harmed person needs to withdraw, reconsider the relationship and assess whether forgiveness can even be a possibility now.

All three types of forgiveness could be available both to the primary victims and to third parties in some way rendered vulnerable by the harm that befell someone with whom they closely identify. My hope is that this analysis, which certainly does not constitute a theory or an explanation of forgiveness, will help survivors, harmers and observers to make sense of the many possible forgiveness trajectories that could open up in the aftermath of serious harm.

It is not about creating watertight categories, but understanding that a wide variety of practices and processes all belong under the heading of forgiveness. This, I believe, is very good news for those who have been harmed and seek to move in a forgiving direction.

15

Whirlpool

The acts of forgiveness that catch the eye of the media are not the private ones. Nor does responsive forgiveness tend to attract attention, emerging as it does from an overture from or extended engagement with the harmer. It is gift forgiveness which grabs our attention, especially in the aftermath of violence. But the giving involved in forgiving raises an issue more insidious than violence itself, which can often lie behind it and be expressed through it. Hatred.

The subject of hatred was raised in Gloria's letter in Chapter 2. She spoke about managing her abusive husband through a complex process of acceptance, retaliation, forgiveness and threat, but absolutely drew the line when it came to forgiving those who hate you. Her letter ended, *There's no excuse for hatred. And no forgiving it either. You just have to stop it.* And yet some of the most well-known and inspiring stories of forgiveness have been when a bereaved person forgives a racist or supremacist murderer, for instance that of Gee Walker mentioned in the last chapter and some of the family members in Charleston in 2015, one of whom, Alanna Simmons, said, 'Although my grandfather and the other victims died at the hands of hate, this is proof that they lived and loved,' she said. 'Hate won't win.'[1]

Such acts of forgiveness are remarkable, controversial and complex. We have already seen how Roxanne Gay stood back and refused to forgive Dylann Roof and Myisha Cherry has argued that the dynamics of racism and oppression mean we need to be alert to the reality of 'racialized forgiveness'.[2] Such a critical perspective would interpret certain acts of forgiveness not as prophetic or transformative acts but as self-fulfilling and self-oppressing prophecies.

However, while there can indeed be an oppressive dynamic at work when the powerless and less privileged forgive the powerful and privileged, such gestures might also have the capacity to change the narrative, assert dignity, reinforce resilience and promote a superior ethical and spiritual mindset.

There is a strand in civil rights thinking that goes back to Howard Thurman and his thoughts about hatred in the context of forgiveness after racially motivated attacks. For Thurman, hatred is one of the 'hounds of hell that dog the footsteps of the disinherited'. Long before psychologists were concerned with the toxic aspects of resentment and 'unforgiveness', Thurman was alert to the self-destructive capacities of hatred. Hatred, he believes, is born of bitterness 'made possible by sustained resentment which is bottled up until it distils an essence of vitality'.[3] Hatred, he is clear, serves a purpose – it 'becomes a device by which an individual seeks to protect himself against moral disintegration'.[4] But he also sees that it is toxic, and 'destroys finally the core of the life of the hater'.[5] Moreover, 'hatred tends to dry up the springs of creative thought in the life of the hater', prompting a preoccupation with 'the negative aspects of his environment'.[6]

Thurman's articulation of the dangers of responding with hatred to oppression, exploitation, attack, abuse or worse became the cornerstone of the civil rights movement under Martin Luther King. An antipathy to hatred, *and* the commitment to allow no place for hate, remain part of the culture of anti-racist communities, as well as behind public expressions of gift forgiveness in certain contexts.

To say this doesn't contradict the concern that the main impact is to create a stereotype of Black acceptance of injustice. Depending on the political and social context, there could even be a case for keeping the non-hating response within the orbit of private forgiveness. When Jane Eyre forgave Mr Rochester, she didn't disclose it to him: she knew him well enough, I would say, to expect that he would immediately seek to exploit her goodwill.

But when racially inspired homicides become matters of public concern and media interest, messages *will* be communicated. The bereaved are confused and vulnerable and potentially very wary of becoming consumed with indignation, anger and resentment, and might fear that in the chaos of it all the hound of hell will take the opportunity to move in. There could, in other words, be a realistic concern of becoming a hater. There could also be a strong desire to offer something positive. To point to another way. To put hope at the epicentre of a storm of despair.

There is undoubtedly genuine giving in such forgiveness, in that it inspires and encourages others. As we saw in Chapter 13, Mina Smallman had already preached about Gee Walker, and remembered her when she herself was bereaved by murder. Gift forgiveness after a violent death is a strong witness against the ethics of retaliation and hatred.

The tension between forgiveness as an alternative to hatred, and forbearing from forgiveness in order to avoid perpetuating oppression, is huge. It is difficult because it represents the same political aim – to move beyond hatred-fuelled racial oppression – but involves the opposite tactics. It *is* good, but it is also *problematic,* to forgive on this racialized script. Is the tension resolvable? I think it might be, but only if we change the way we think and talk about forgiveness. Once again we see a problem for the harmed caused by the over-simplification of forgiveness, and its over-promotion as the most admirable (because most costly) and best possible response by someone who has been harmed.

What we lack is a way of describing the non-retaliatory, non-vengeful, hate-avoiding response to having been harmed, without straying into the territory of either reporting or delivering forgiveness; of responding with dignity and peaceableness while eschewing any suggestion of, 'I have forgiven' or, 'I now forgive.'

We need to build into our repertoire of post-harm responses a deep yet pragmatic sense of the vital importance of *hope*; to give the harmed permission to recognize that they are in a moment of clock-stopping crisis, but that they remain inhabitants of time. Therefore, they don't need to do everything in this moment – hyperreal though it probably seems. Cruelly bereaved believers should be encouraged to have a sense of God not as sitting back waiting for them to forgive, but rather embracing their loved one, and holding the hands of all who grieve. The faintest idea that the Almighty might be waiting to hear the bereaved forgive could create a terrible form of forgiveness-pressure. So too could be the half-remembered pulpit message of grievously harmed victims heroically forgiving, or the biblical threats made to those who will not forgive – even up to seventy times seven. And, worst of all, the inaccurate but relentlessly repeated myth that Jesus forgave from the cross, thereby setting an example for us all.

We have seen how an expression of hope can make the request to be forgiven acceptable. To express one's attitude towards a person who has inflicted grievous harm in terms of hope can, I suggest, open the door to a much less problematic way of connecting serious harmers with the possibility of forgiveness.

It doesn't deal with the fact the relatives of Black people killed by racists are likely to be asked if they forgive, whereas those of victims killed by Black people are not asked the forgiveness question. But complex as the reasons for that bias are, the situation can only improve if a way of peaceably responding to grievous harm can be developed which doesn't rely on a simplistic model or declaratory tone with regard to forgiveness. The less forgiveness in a crisis is driven by forgiveness-anxiety or forgiveness-pressure, and a fingers-crossed optimism that the forgiver today will be an equally confident forgiver in the future, the more realistic our expectations of all those who have suffered serious harm will be.

Some people *will* be ready to offer gift forgiveness in a moment of grievous crisis, and a broad view of forgiveness allows us to appreciate that it might mean a variety of things. For some to say, 'I forgive you' or, 'I have forgiven him,' will be a statement of the absolute inner truth that they have eradicated anger, bitterness, hatred and moral debt; that they no longer 'hold anything against' and have nothing but goodwill towards, the perpetrator. For others, a statement of forgiveness might be more of a vow or a commitment or a promise. Not a naïve, 'I have got over it,' but a strong, 'I shall overcome the power of hatred and I shall not act out of the anger and vengefulness that I now feel.' For others, a public statement might be more delicately poised, and have the simpler meaning that they are taking a stand against retaliation and vengeance and thereby offering an alternative to the cycle of violence.

Such variety is realistic and acceptable, but still vulnerable to the criticism that it is giving away too much; that, in its contribution to a social pattern of instances, it subtly undermines important values like equality and justice.

What I am looking for are ways of recognizing the reality of grievous loss and the moral outrage, anger and disorientation that violent death must bring, while honouring the need to find a way to hold off that hound of hell known as hatred. This is a hugely important challenge. Some people at least know that the moment of loss and vulnerability is also the moment when others might listen. And some who have long been battling against forces of hatred and oppression will naturally see this as an opportunity to inhabit and proclaim the highest values, and commit to paying the price – by absorbing all the collateral effects of such damage themselves. This is genuinely admirable and humbling. But there may be ways to assert and proclaim all the highest values without taking a step too far with forgiveness, and risking deflecting public and political attention from the moral outrage that is appropriate.

So: what might be said by a person who has been bereaved by a racist hate crime, who is not minded to be vengeful or stoop to hatred, but feels that to offer forgiveness at this moment might be to give too much away. Here is my best suggestion.

> *I am grieving for my loss. That my son's life was taken from him with terrible violence by a person who hates people of colour is something that chills me to the core of my being. But I will not respond to violence and hatred with either violence or hatred. I hope one day that I will be able to say that I have forgiven, but there is too much grief and anger in my heart now to say that.*
>
> *As for the perpetrators, I hope they will come to understand the evil of what they have done <u>and</u> of the hatred they harbour. When they do, they may perhaps appreciate the forgiveness of a grievously and cruelly bereaved mother, and I hope that by then I will be in a position to give it. But I am not giving it to a person who hates people like me.*

I make this bold suggestion not to put words in anyone's mouth but to offer something that might take away some of the pressure to forgive that can sometimes be a terrible burden. A balance is needed. We should not only encourage people to be forgiving but to be honest and straightforward when they can't forgive. To do that involves identifying, enlarging and populating the space between vengeance and hatred on the one side, and forgiveness on the other. One way we can do that is by finding ways to celebrate and honour those whose reality is in this ambiguous and yet human space of non-vengeful unforgiveness.

Although harmed in very different ways and not in racially motivated crimes, both Michael Lapsley and Marian Partington can be thought of as inhabiting this in-between or liminal space. Michael was almost killed and severely injured when a letter bomb blew off his hands. As we saw in Chapter 13, he has written that in more recent years his heart has softened towards the bomber. He does not desire revenge and has no hatred, but he has not forgiven.

Marian Partington's younger sister Lucy was a student of English Literature, a poet and artist, and a recent convert to Roman Catholicism when she was abducted by the serial killers Fredrick and Rosemary West. Marian's book *If You Sit Very Still* is a searing yet hopeful autobiographical reflection on, first, coming to terms with Lucy's unexplained disappearance and then, 20 years later, living with the truth that her remains had been found buried in the grounds of 25 Cromwell Street, Gloucester, along with those of nine other murdered girls and women.

In her book, Marian narrates her journey with loss, bewilderment, rage, anguish, self-discovery, spirituality and forgiveness. She explains that it was in the context of carefully guided Chan Buddhist retreats that she began to explore her inner pain, which she called 'the frozen'.

She identified four possible ways forward: denying it, dumping it on others, 'letting it corrode me' and, to her own surprise, forgiving. This, it seemed to her, was 'the most imaginative, creative way forward'. She has subsequently told me that she 'didn't like the word nor understand how it could come about', but that 'the vow to line myself up for it was a very strong intention. It was about choosing to be alive.'

Marian's journey has been lengthy and complex. Her memoir is shockingly honest in its revelation of how she was able to make a connection with Rosemary West. Shortly after the retreat at which she vowed to forgive she was overwhelmed by feelings of murderous rage. This was not focused on the Wests but a deeper, more generic, overwhelming and, as she once put it to me, 'purifying' experience. Marian has also written about the way in which silence (solitary and shared), spiritual guidance, attending to significant dreams and Quaker and Chan Buddhist practices, were all integral to the erosion in her of the 'self-centred delusion of being separate and superior'. This in turn led to the sense that the gulf between her and Rosemary West was not so great after all. And in 2004 she wrote her a letter.

All this took a great deal of time. Twenty years passed between Lucy's death and the discovery of her body in Gloucester. It was then a year before Marian went on her second retreat and thereafter had her encounter with murderous rage. Nine years later, in 2004, she wrote a letter for Rosemary West, but she didn't send it for a further four years.

Marian's letter, which is printed in full in her memoir, is remarkable in many ways, and incorporates some beautiful images and profound insights. It rehearses the facts that are known and expresses the hope that Rosemary is receiving the help she needs to come to terms with her past. These extracts connect with our exploration of what forgiving involves.

> I have been seeking to know how to be free of any feelings of anger and bitterness towards you.
>
> At last I can write to tell you something that you may not understand but which may help you too in some way. I can honestly say that at times I feel a strange sort of gratitude towards you, because I have had to face myself as a human being, deep inside. Now I know a true compassion for the terrible suffering that you have created by your actions, for yourself and so many other people.
>
> When I vowed to try to forgive you on my first Chan retreat . . . I experienced murderous rage shortly afterwards. Somehow I knew that I could have killed someone too. My inner work began in earnest. I realized that I need to train myself to lessen the harm that I can do to my own life and the lives of others by facing my own greed, hatred and ignorance . . .
>
> I am sending you these words in the hope that they may help you in some way. Please know that I do not feel any hostility towards you; just a sadness, a deep sadness that all this has happened, and that your heart could not feel a truth that I wish you could know.
>
> Our lives are connected . . . May you be less burdened by fear.[7]

The only reply was from the prison authorities, to say that Ms West had asked that Marian 'please cease all correspondence'.

Marian's letter makes it clear that she has engaged in both the positive and negative aspects of private and gift forgiveness. Among the many noteworthy aspects are that she prepared so assiduously before venturing to make a gift of forgiveness. But it is also helpful to note both the extent of what she offers in the letter and its modesty and restraint. There is assurance that there is no anger or bitterness, mention of 'a strange sort of gratitude', recognition that Rosemary West has caused suffering for herself as well as others, an almost casual reference to the vow to try to forgive ('when I vowed . . .'), acknowledgement that she, Marian, needed to 'lessen the harm that I can do', clarification that she has no hostility, but that deep sadness remains, and, finally, an affirmation of connectedness and an expression of goodwill, blessing almost, in the words, 'may you be less burdened by fear'.

There is dignity, honesty and integrity in Marian's acknowledgement of shared humanity with Rosemary, and her confession that she could imagine taking a life. And there is a combination of extraordinary aspiration and manifest humility in the words, 'I vowed to try to forgive you.' All this connects profoundly with the argument that has been developing here, of the centrality that the quality of hope has in moving and motivating the harmed towards forgiveness. I find it hard to imagine anything more gracious or inspiring.

If we attend closely to stories of forgiveness, we might sometimes notice that the forgiver finds themself in this space *between* vengefulness, hatred or bitterness and a form of forgiveness that is considered to be complete, pardoning or closed: non-vengeful unforgiveness. It is an important, honourable, realistic and yet complicated and ambiguous space, with its own geography and dynamism. Language does not stand still here. I have described it in a doubly negative way, but for some it will be understood as a form of forgiveness – forgiveness being seen as the avoidance of revenge or the eschewing of hatred. One person's unforgiveness really can be another person's forgiveness.

Part of this book's plea is that the truth of the ambiguity, complexity and dynamism of this space be appreciated and attempts made to describe it. This is a complex space where the harmer is met by the harmed person's desire neither to be captured by the poison of their own resentment, nor to diminish by retaliating in kind, and yet is determined not to give them a free pass by failing in the moral duty of naming, shaming and responding with apt emotion to egregious and harming actions and the attitudes that motivate them. The plea is also that we applaud those who manage to move away from vengefulness and hatred, yet know they have not reached the far shore of happy forgiveness but only entered into this different, inherently fluid, space. An ocean, perhaps, with ebbs and flows, rip currents and waves; or a river with rapids and eddies, deeps and shallows.

No wonder that to enter the debate about forgiveness is, as I said in the introduction, to be swept into a whirlpool. Forgiving after serious harm or in the context of hatred is *dynamic*, uncertain and likely to be forever unfinished, whatever labels we put on the various steps people might be able to make. But these hard-won insights into the fluid creativity of forgiving – so important to those who have been harmed – can be lost when we allow the divine forgiveness of sinners to be our paradigm, or think that the playground model still applies, when the abstraction of the noun 'forgiveness' shapes our thinking, and when naïve optimism suggests that if only we could decisively forgive our harmers we would be healed from the wounds and traumas they have inflicted.

Forgiveness after trauma is not closure; it is an ongoing, potentially perilous journey. After serious, life-changing harm the question is not, 'Have you forgiven?' It is, 'Do you hope to forgive?' Or, to continue our metaphor, 'Are you standing on the solid rock of vengefulness or hatred, or have you, in hope, risked entering the dangerous waters where the forgivers swim?'

III

RESPONSES

16

Replies

The letters from imagined readers in Chapter 2 trenchantly suggested that there really were limits to forgiveness. That's a challenging notion, but it must be clear by now that a suitable reply from me would not be along the following lines.

> *Thank you for your message. Let me assure you that forgiveness is always good, despite the passionate feelings sometimes felt by those who have been very badly treated. So I suggest you are worrying unnecessarily. Forgiveness is always ultimately possible, and Christianity has all the answers. Forgiveness takes time, to be sure, sometimes a lot of time, and so it's important to be patient with yourself. It may be difficult to imagine now, but one day its time will come. You'll get there!*

No, that is not what I've been arguing, and it cannot be the conclusion. The answer to the question in this book's title is not a negative. Both forgiveness and the unforgivable remain on the table.

Here, then, are attempts to reply to the letters. First, David, whose daughter was abandoned by her husband when she was dying of a degenerative disease.

Dear David

May I express my sincere condolences. I can't imagine the agony you've been through as a father. Fergal Keane once wrote that 'There is nothing in my world so terrifying as the thought that harm will be wrought on my child, and nothing so sure as my sense that the hope for vengeance would live with me for ever.' I think we can all relate to that.

I'm sure that your son's advice that you consider forgiving was well intended, and maybe he has seen people move on from intense anger and bitterness before. But I must confess I was intrigued that he likened your situation to the biblical story of the Prodigal Son. I'm not sure I saw many parallels myself. I read that story as about a lost son being welcomed home, though first, of course, he had to find his true self, which he did when things went wrong for him and he was at his lowest ebb. It's certainly not a story about a father deciding not to feel any anger or bitterness towards the young man who by his choices had so grievously let himself and his father down.

I wonder whether it is possible to imagine something that might bring your situation closer to the Prodigal Son story? This would have to start with your son-in-law coming to an understanding of what he's done and the harm and the suffering it's caused.

The second part would be for him to feel he should make a journey back to see you and say something. But what? This is where the Bible story helps, and suggests to me that if he really does come to his senses he will say something like this: 'I have come to say that I now regret most deeply the way I treated your daughter and you. No words of apology would be adequate, and I ask nothing of you. But I want you to know that as I have got older I have come to a deeper understanding of how atrocious my behaviour was. I don't ask your forgiveness. I will not forgive myself. I am grateful that you listened to me. I don't want to cause you any further grief, but I wanted you to know that and to say it in person.'

David, you are not in the same position as the father in that Bible story and should feel no obligation to forgive. But sometimes people do have a deep change of heart, and if they do, some other things might also change.

As things stand I don't think he's unforgivable, but we have to believe, or if not believe then hope against hope, that even the people who have done the most disloyal and hurtful things in the past may one day come to an unblinkered understanding of their responsibilities, and seek not to put things right, but simply let it be known that they now understand how atrocious their behaviour was.

Thank you for writing. It's a terrible loss you've sustained. I can't imagine what you've been through.

We turn now to Gloria, who found ways of coping with an abusive husband but rejected any possibility of forgiving someone who hated her.

Dear Gloria

Thank you so much for writing to me with your thoughts about forgiveness. I can see you have found a way of managing your domestic situation, and I hope it is enabling you to feel safe and fulfilled. Only you will know, and I am sure you are able to make good decisions.

The question you raise – whether you can forgive someone you know hates you – is a very important one. You may be surprised to hear that I mostly agree with you. I certainly don't think anyone should ever set out to persuade you that you should forgive them.

The big question, of course, is what you mean by 'forgive'. Certainly I agree it's impossible to say to someone you know hates you that 'I forgive you for hating me.' It just doesn't make sense.

What does make sense when someone hates you, however, is not to stoop to their level. Not to hate the hater back. This is what the Obamas mean when they say, 'When they go low, we go high.' It's recognizing that hating doesn't need to be responded to with either hatred or forgiveness, but maybe something which isn't either. Something in the space between.

But what you say about forgiveness in the course of a loving relationship is so true. If you really love someone and know that they love you, there is motivation to forgive and to set love back on its course again.

That doesn't mean we have to put up with anything. To riff slightly on your question: you have said you can't forgive someone who hates you – can you in any meaningful sense forgive someone who doesn't respect you?

Anyway, thank you again for writing. I'm sorry I can't answer all your searching questions, and I am sure you are right that God is justice and truth – but let me add mercy and peace as well. The question for us to figure out is how all that fits together in our everyday lives and relationships. May God bless you, sister, as you go forward in faith and hope. But, Gloria, I hope things really are OK at home.

Now Michael, the former terrorist from Northern Ireland who had turned against any possibility that he might be forgiven.

Dear Michael

Thank you so much for taking the trouble to write to me. I guess we are of a similar age!

I have a lot of sympathy with what you say. The reality of the harm that people inflict through violence and terrorism isn't something that can be eradicated by forgiveness. And I can see why you feel that the stain on your being caused by your murderous actions is something you will always have to live with.

I was most struck by how you implacably reject any form of forgiveness for yourself, whether it's God's or your victims', the survivors of your victims, or you own self-forgiveness. It might sound odd, but I want to applaud you for that. You're recognizing the gravity of what you were responsible for and saying 'no' to any easy answers. Quite right.

But what are you going to do, Michael? From what you've written I don't think you can do any more to acknowledge what you've done. But maybe there is some way you can be involved in some peacemaking work, or perhaps do some volunteering in a Protestant area. You can't make good the damage you caused, but maybe you can do some small thing that would make life a bit easier or better or more promising for someone else. Forget about forgiveness. Forget about doing anything that could earn forgiveness. Think about service.

One final thing. Yes, I agree. We should think of men like you as former child soldiers. Your childhood and young adulthood were taken away from you by force, but don't let the people who exploited you then rob you of any chance of fulfilment in your senior years. Think forwards, Michael. The past isn't going to change, but maybe you don't need to hold on to your anger and bitterness quite so tenaciously?

Look, it was good to get your letter, and if you want to write again I'd be glad to hear from you. And let's be on first-name terms.

Finally, Ingabere from Rwanda, who rejected Bishop Tutu's message of forgiveness and reconciliation.

Dear Ingabere

I can't believe you were kind enough to write to me from Rwanda. I send you warm greetings.

Yes, I had read about Bishop Tutu's visit to your country and the response to his words about forgiveness and reconciliation. What I think I learned from it was that, whenever we talk about situations in which people have behaved terribly and caused suffering, we need to remember that every situation is different. Bishop Tutu had a huge role to play in helping his own country make a very difficult political transition. And I'm not surprised that he and other people were keen to share the lessons they had learned in the process. After all, if they had discovered exactly what it is that turns evil into good, or harm into harmony – well, it would be very mean if they kept that secret to themselves.

But it turns out that there is no secret, no magic potion, no alchemy that can be universally applied to heal and reconcile after atrocious harm has been inflicted. On the other hand, I really do believe people like Tutu are right to say that we all need to find ways of responding to violence that are not full of vengefulness. But it might be more helpful just to say, 'Let's avoid vengeance,' rather than, 'Let's forgive and reconcile.'

Can I be straightforward with you, Ingabere? I don't know how seriously you meant the words 'Lord have mercy' in your letter to me, but I feel they might be exactly the right words after atrocious harm has been committed. Of course, the brutal, disgusting, genocidal massacres of your country were times when no mercy at all was shown. Maybe the true lesson to be taken from this awful reality is that we must somehow never stop wanting and hoping and working for a world where there is mercy. And even if we don't feel merciful ourselves, we can maybe pray for mercy and hope that such merciless days will never be seen again.

17

UNFORGIVABLE?

In this final chapter I offer a response to Chris Green, the imagined abuse victim whose mother had been murdered, and who invited me to reflect more deeply about forgiveness and the unforgivable.

Dear Chris

Thank you indeed for writing to me. Your letter touched me deeply and made me think profoundly. This reply is just the tip of the iceberg of what I have been thinking since you wrote!

You asked me whether I think that Christianity has got forgiveness right?

Short answer – no, it hasn't. Forgiveness is such a complicated and personal matter that there will always be mistakes and misunderstandings in theory and practice. But Christianity needs to do better. Let me make that more specific by setting out six pleas to Christian leaders.

1 *Stop basing your ideas of what's appropriate in interpersonal forgiveness on beliefs about how God forgives. Some philosophers have spoken about forgiveness being a 'power' of victims.*

But you don't become God when you are abused: you become even more vulnerable. We need to stop thinking of forgiveness as a power and think of it as human grace that flows not out of duty or even response but out of absolute freedom. It is only free forgiveness that is truly forgiveness. The first task is not to persuade people to forgive but to help them to be free.

2. *Appreciate the huge difference between forgiveness after low-impact harms and the unintentional consequences of well-intended decisions, and serious, life-changing and traumatic harms. And understand that Jesus's message about forgiving over and over again and not being mean to people when you have been in receipt of generosity is only relevant at this first, lower level.*
3. *Stop saying that Jesus regularly forgave people, in the sense that he routinely offered interpersonal forgiveness. It's true that he offered God's forgiveness and that he didn't retaliate. But these actions are different from the forgiveness of someone who has been personally harmed.*
4. *Wise up about forgiveness-anxiety and find ways of steering both victims and perpetrators away from it. This will involve great care in how forgiveness is praised and promoted.*
5. *Recognize that the priority for abusers and others who have inflicted harm should not be to seek forgiveness but to repent.*
6. *Recognize that remorse is largely irrelevant to victims and that apologies making a point*

of stressing emotion are inappropriate and unhelpful.

I hope these points are plain enough, but I want to say a bit more about forgiveness-anxiety, repentance and remorse. First, forgiveness-anxiety. Christianity is proud of its reputation as a religion of forgiveness, and many of its leaders feel a responsibility to explain and promote interpersonal forgiving. Some push forgiveness forward as a duty, imperative or obligation.

The sexual abuse crisis has led to a good deal of rowing back from this position and seen important pronouncements that no one must be pressured or forced to forgive. For instance, 'guidelines' recently produced to support the Anglican Church around the world acknowledge that 'Forgiveness is one of the most difficult issues faced by victims and church workers who minister to victims and abusers.' Further, that 'Victims often find themselves under pressure to forgive the abuser.

'Victims must never be pressured by church workers to forgive their abuser. Further harm can be caused to a victim through pressure to forgive, and re-establish their relationship with their abuser. They may condemn themselves and believe they are condemned by others if they are not willing, or able to forgive. They may see themselves as 'not being Christian' and beyond the forgiveness of God.'[1]

This is very helpful, but the guidelines don't say much about internal pressure – or about what it means not to forgive. And that's where I feel more work needs to be done.

Pressure to forgive can build up in subtle and strange ways. For instance, while people who offer forgiveness after terrible harm has been inflicted can be encouraging and inspiring, praising and promoting them can add to the pressure on people who can't forgive.

This external pressure can create or exacerbate the tension that people experience when they feel they should forgive but know they can't – 'forgiveness-anxiety'. My worry is that, despite its best intentions to be victim-friendly, Christianity generates a lot of forgiveness-anxiety.

It isn't only victims who experience forgiveness-anxiety: it's perpetrators. But whereas victims worry about not forgiving, the perpetrator worries about not being forgiven. What, then, should be said to perpetrators? This is where 'repentance' comes in.

The guidelines I mentioned include a section on 'repentance', which addresses what a perpetrator of abuse needs to do if they want to be forgiven by God. But there isn't a section on what they're meant to do if they want to be forgiven by the person they abused. Worse, there isn't a section which steps back and asks questions such as, 'What is it appropriate for the person who has abused others to want and hope for?'

I want guidelines that help an abuser recognize that repentance is of value in its own right, not something you need to do in order to be forgiven by God. The best things a perpetrator can do are acknowledge what they have done, seek to understand its impact on others, accept the punishment, take whatever steps they can to avoid any risk of doing it again, and come up with some practical ideas about making amends.

That little list is what I think 'repentance' really means. It's a change process that is appropriate and valuable in its own right, not a forgiveness-seeking process.

Christianity needs to move on from giving the impression that there are things you can do to get forgiveness. No: there are things you can do to make the world a better place tomorrow (but not yesterday), and if you do some of them you may become more forgivable – or maybe less unforgivable. Ultimately forgiveness is something that the harmed person may or may not engage in. They may forgive in an inner quiet way that helps them but is not communicated; they may forgive by letting the harmer know that they have forgiven or hope to be able to forgive in the future. And they may forgive in response to some communication from the harmer.

After abuse, it's the third of these that is tricky, because the harmed person needs to be confident that the harmer is sincere, and that they are not reconnecting in a manipulative way. That's always going to be difficult. Abusers are controllers. They use their position and power in inappropriate ways and for selfish ends. They will use anything available. They are exploiters and schemers, and they should not be forgiven for abusing unless they've given up exploiting and scheming. It may seem paradoxical, but dropping all efforts to gain forgiveness would be a reasonable sign of such a change. If an abuser were to reach out to their victims, the appropriate message might be: 'I recognize now how I abused the trust and power I had over you and profoundly regret the suffering that this has caused you. I have no right to expect anything from you, and thank you for reading this note.'

That might sound very unemotional, but that's the point. The last thing the abuser should do is push their emotional agenda on to their victim. And they should definitely not ask to be forgiven, as that is to project their own forgiveness-anxiety and heighten the victim's.

Christianity has not been cautious enough about remorse. For instance, the Anglican Church authorities allowed the church youth worker and child sex abuser Timothy Storey 'to continue working with children after "expressing remorse for everything he had done wrong"'.[2] *The tragedy and scandal was not only what was going on in Storey's mind but also that the relevant church authorities were convinced by his expressions of remorse that he should be trusted again. Ultimately Storey was sentenced to 15 years for what he had done: three counts of rape and one count of assault by penetration – all on teenagers he had encountered in his youth ministry and manipulated, groomed and coerced.*

Let me be clear. If a perpetrator seeks forgiveness from God and has no remorse, then they are going about things the wrong way. If, however, a perpetrator seeks to do the right thing by a person they have abused, then they need to engage in the sort of repentance that I have outlined and forget advertising how bad they feel.

This sounds like a message to abusers, but it's actually a message to the abused. You are right to be wary of remorse. If it comes from someone who has exploited your trust in the past it is unwise and maybe even irresponsible to take it at face value. It's acknowledgement that matters.

You also asked whether you should take any further steps towards forgiving the man who murdered your mother. It seems to me from what you have said that you have moved on emotionally from your initial feelings. You are not plotting revenge and, as far as I can make out, you don't hate him. What matters most here, I think, is how you are going to remember your mother over the months and years to come. If you think it would honour her memory in some way to find out more about the man who killed her then maybe that would be something to explore. But it's really a question of what you feel your priorities are in your spiritual and emotional journey going forward.

The other thing I'd mention here is that if you do feel any forgiveness-anxiety with regard to the murderer, remember that the only forgiveness you could ever offer would be for what he has done to you by killing your mother. You are not in a position to forgive on her behalf – or on behalf of anyone else.

If you want to look forward several years, you might want to think about how you would feel should you hear that the murderer has been released from prison. You might be struck by the injustice that he is now free of the consequences of his actions, whereas you and other members of your mother's family are not. That could be testing for you, but I don't have any particular advice about how to handle it – other than that it might be best to anticipate it.

Finally, you asked me why I didn't write about sexual abuse in my first book, and you suggested it might have been because secretly I thought it was unforgivable. I think you have me there. I have been very reluctant to think in terms of people being unforgivable, but recognize I need to come off the fence and say that, yes, people can become unforgivable. Let me briefly explain why.

We say that people are 'unforgivable' when we are in the process of absorbing news of especially egregious and cruel harm. At such times to call it unforgivable, or to refrain from mentioning forgiveness, is a way of marking the gravity of the offence and expressing solidarity with the victims and survivors. This does not imply that revenge should be taken, though this is what some who see others as unforgivable would feel like doing.

But a truly unforgivable person is someone who not only has inflicted terrible harm but also denies and disputes it, or seeks to minimize or even justify it. What makes them unforgivable is more than the absence of repentance: it is the presence of an attitude that makes repentance impossible. An unforgivable person's actions have put them beyond any norms of relating or relational or ethical repair. There is a vacancy around them where ethical and relational connection would normally be found. Another way of putting this is to say that people can behave in such a way as to make the forgivability gap infinitely wide, to the extent that no one, no victim, no survivor, no observer or bystander, can bridge it. In such circumstances the harmed may try to let go of their resentment and maybe even just stop harrowing themselves over it. But even if they get somewhere with that, I don't think this means the harmer has been forgiven.

One reason why we do not like the idea that some people are unforgivable is that we might think it obliges us to hate them. I am not sure this is true, but I do think it is sometimes right to let ourselves hate someone. And so I don't feel it is right to criticize anyone who hates the person who abused them as a child, or those who may have exacerbated their suffering by disbelieving or minimizing it. It is costly to hate, and good to move on from it but to say that hatred is never appropriate is, I think, to fail to understand how deeply people can be harmed, and how outrageous it is for certain kinds of behaviours not to be sanctioned. What matters is that a person who hates is aware of their hatred, able to use it effectively and not be trapped by it. If a person is to be free to forgive, however, that freedom needs to include the freedom to hate.

Is it right to designate abusers as unforgivable? I think so. Partly for the positive reason that to call someone unforgivable is to stop short of calling them a monster. As many people have pointed out, if you call someone a monster you let them off the hook of responsibility. Only a responsible human being can be unforgivable, because only a responsible human being can be forgiven.

There is another reason why we might feel it is right to say that an abuser is unforgivable. This has to do not with the physical or sexual aspects of abuse, but rather the exploiting of trust, position and access, and the processes of manipulation and trust-building that are labelled 'grooming'. This is true of all sexual abuse, but the abuse of children is different again, because it inflicts on the innocent experiences and treacheries that are incomprehensible to them, and which disturb them in ways they are not able to understand or rectify. This is why it is outrageous to talk of forgiveness in the context of the sexual abuse of children.

Seriously abusive behaviours break down the norms of relating, and cause people not only to have a traumatic experience but also lose the confidence to place the trust in others on which society and relationships depend. People become unforgivable when their behaviour undermines the psychological and spiritual fundamentals that make a positively forward-looking life possible, whether that is by understanding others or understanding ourselves. Unforgivable harms are not egregious harms in the past, but insidious harms which corrupt the future. This is why I agree with those who say that the unforgivable is that which kills hope.[3] *If a harming action is a hope-killing action, then the perpetrator moves themself beyond the realm of forgivability. They make the forgivability gap far too wide to be bridged.*

Can a human being forgive the unforgivable?

I think this can become possible, but only if something happens to rekindle or resurrect those aspects of the harmed person that were killed or corrupted or disfigured by the harming actions. If things happen that allow the people in whom hope has been killed to hope again then, it seems to me, forgiveness might once again become a possibility. The question then is, what could conceivably happen that might resurrect hope? And that, as you might have guessed, brings us back to repentance;

not in the remorse-laden sense but in the sense of acknowledging, taking responsibility and recognizing that it is impossible to make amends.

But what about God? Is God able to forgive the unforgivable? Does God ever draw a line and say, 'No, you cannot be forgiven?' The truth to my mind is somewhere between the two. No, God is not in a position to forgive someone who has inflicted life-changing, hope-shattering harm 'just like that'. God does, however, have the capacity to respond to repentance. But what God should be interested in, if I may speak to God, is not whether or not any confession of sins has the appropriate tone of remorsefulness or contrition, but whether or not the abuser has repented in the sense I have been describing.

In such extreme situations, therefore, the standard Christian tropes about forgiving quickly and repeatedly are not applicable, and when it comes to forgiveness God takes second place to the victim. If an abuser does the right thing by the victim, then they move away from being unforgivable. If they don't – they don't.

So, in short, Chris, yes, some people are unforgivable.

ACKNOWLEDGEMENTS

My gratitude flows to all whose books and articles about forgiveness I have read, to those who have been trusting and kind enough to share and discuss their own experiences with me, and to those who in conversation or by email exchange have both stretched my thinking and encouraged me to think more.

I have gained a great deal from Anthony Bash, Marina Cantacuzino and Marian Partington, and record my gratitude to them all for their remarkable contributions in this area, and for their friendship.

In the summer of 2021 three King's students, Ama Dragomir, Emily Hyde and KC Onuoroa, spent six weeks engaging with me on the question of how forgiveness theories and forgiveness stories connect. Our long daily conversations were intense and wide-ranging and an important part of the gestation of this book. I am grateful to them, and to Kayla Robins, who joined us for part of the time, for their enthusiasm and divergent insights.

Forgiveness is a word to be handled with care – and so too is the concept of the unforgivable. There is an almost sacred responsibility when talking or writing about forgiveness towards those who, having been harmed or having inflicted great harm, have found solace in forgiveness together with those for whom, for whatever reason, forgiveness has not been presented sympathetically or broadly enough to be an option worth considering. But the responsibility towards those who have brought the idea and possibility of forgiveness into healing dialogue with their worst experiences is huge. Nonetheless, it feels to me inevitable that whatever is written about someone's experience of serious harm and journey towards (or away from) forgiveness will always be in some way inadequate. So much depends on word choice, tone, detail and nuance. I can only hope that the inevitable errors are not hurtful to them or misleading to others.

One of the remarkable and sustaining things about working on the question of the limits of forgiveness is the immediacy and seriousness of engagement it elicited from almost everyone to whom I have mentioned it. This book has sometimes been an isolating and lonely venture – as is any writing – but mention the limits of forgiveness in conversation and many will quickly engage. I have no doubt that the issues raised when probing these limits will have exercised and perplexed many people as they have observed the hurts and harms inflicted on others, or tried to cope with experiences that have wounded and damaged them, or indeed the knowledge that they are responsible for or complicit with harm that others have suffered. They are difficult to talk about; disturb sleep; lie behind the headlines far more often than we realize. If you are one of them, and you have read my words, I am grateful to you.

Finally, I am grateful to my beloved Maggie at home, my close colleagues at King's, to Robin Baird-Smith and his team at Bloomsbury Continuum for their forbearance as well as their generous encouragement, guidance and trust, and to Graham Coster of Safe Haven Books for his assiduous and patient work as copy editor.

NOTES

Introduction

1 'Dianna Ortiz, American Nun Tortured in Guatemala, Dies at 62', *New York Times* 20 February 2021; www.nytimes.com/2021/02/20/us/dianna-ortiz-dead.html. See also 'Dianna Ortiz, nun who told of brutal abduction by Guatemalan military, dies at 62' *Washington Post*, 19 February 2021; www.washingtonpost.com/local/obituaries/dianna-ortiz-nun-who-told-of-brutal-abduction-by-guatemalan-military-dies-at-62/2021/02/19/932ac25a-713a-11eb-85fa-e0ccb3660358_story.html.
2 In an interview in 1997 (see *Washington Post* article above), Sister Ortiz said, 'I am not sure what it means to forgive.'
3 Choice of words is significant when dealing with the aftermath of harm, and there are subtleties and nuances involved in using words like 'victim' and 'survivor'. Rather than debating issues of the most suitable noun I have decided to use whichever of these words seems most appropriate in each sentence, but also to refer to the more neutral 'the harmed' whenever reasonable. Similarly, I refer to harmers, perpetrators or offenders as seems appropriate, without intending to imply anything that is not explicit or implicit in the everyday meaning of such words.
4 Brontë, Charlotte, *Jane Eyre* (1847). Both this quotation and the next one are from Chapter 27.

1. Abuse

1 Cherry, Stephen (2012), *Healing Agony: Re-imagining Forgiveness*. London: Continuum.
2 The Anglican Church Investigation Report | IICSA Independent Inquiry into Child Sexual Abuse.

3 'Forget culture. It's a new theology we need', *Church Times*, 6 April 2018; www.churchtimes.co.uk/articles/2018/6-april/comment/opinion/iicsa-forget-culture-new-theology-we-need.
4 Stein, Josephine Anne (2019), 'Safeguarding Policy at a Crossroads' in Janet and Glio Fife, eds, *Letters to a Broken Church*. London: Ekklesia, 166.
5 Cantacuzino, Marina (2022), *Forgiveness: An Exploration*. London: Simon and Schuster, 256.

3. Promise

1 Lewis, C. S. (1952), *Mere Christianity*. London: Fontana, 101.
2 Worthington, Everett, ed. (2005), *Handbook of Forgiveness*. London: Routledge, 1.
3 Smedes, Lewis (1984), *Forgive and Forget: Healing the Hurts We Don't Deserve*, New York: Harper Row, xii.

4. Fascination

1 Lomax, Eric (1996), *The Railway Man*. London: Vintage.
2 Cassatly, Stephanie (2017), *Notice of Release: A Daughter's Journey to Forgive Her Mother's Killer*. Electio.
3 Kahmisa, Azim (1998), *From Murder to Forgiveness: A Father's Journey*. Bloomington: Balboa Press.
4 Carr, Camilla and James, Jonathan (2008), *The Sky is Always There: Surviving a Kidnap in Chechnya*. London: Canterbury Press, 253.
5 Brison, Susan (2003), *Aftermath: Violence and the Remaking of a Self*. Princeton: Princeton University Press.
6 Thordis Elva and Tom Stranger, 'Our story of rape and reconciliation', TED Talk.
7 Elva, Thordis, and Stranger, Tom (2017), *South of Forgiveness: A True Story of Rape and Responsibility*. Melbourne: Scribe, 261–2.
8 Ibid., 294.
9 Ibid., 250.
10 The Forgiveness Project; www.theforgivenessproject.com/.

11 Schwarzenegger Pratt, Katherine (2020), *The Gift of Forgiveness: Inspiring Stories from Those Who Have Overcome the Unforgivable*. New York: Viking.
12 Ibid., 3.
13 Ibid.

5. Controversy

1 Stevenson, Shelagh (2008), *The Long Road*. London: Methuen Drama.
2 Shaffer, Peter (1993), *The Gift of the Gorgon*. London: Viking, 54.
3 Raine, Nina (2017), *Consent*. London: Nick Hern Books.
4 Hawes, Jennifer Berry (2019), *Grace Will Lead Us Home: The Charleston Church Massacre and the Hard, Inspiring Journey to Forgiveness*. New York: St Martin's Press, 74.
5 'Opinion | Why I Can't Forgive Dylann Roof', *New York Times*, 23 June 2015; www.nytimes.com/2015/06/24/opinion/why-i-cant-forgive-dylann-roof.html.
6 Levi, Primo (2000), *If This is a Man, The Truce*. London: Everyman's Library, 458.

6. Tutu

1 Tutu, Desmond (1999), *No Future Without Forgiveness*. London: Rider.
2 Derrida, Jacques (2002), *On Cosmopolitanism and Forgiveness*. London: Routledge, 42.
3 Van Dijkhuizen, Jan Frans (2018), *A Literary History of Reconciliation: Power, Remorse and the Limits of Reconciliation*. London: Bloomsbury, 16.
4 Enns, Diane (2012), *The Violence of Victimhood*. Philadelphia: Pennsylvania State University Press, 162.
5 Tutu, Desmond & Mpho (2014), *The Book of Forgiving: The Fourfold Path for Healing Ourselves and Our World*. William Collins.
6 Ibid., 56.
7 Ibid., 57.
8 Ibid., 57.

9 Cherry, Myisha (2023), *The Failures of Forgiveness: What We Get Wrong and How to Do Better*. Princeton: Princeton University Press, 67–69.
10 Tutu Van Furth, Mpho (2002), *Forgiveness and Reparation, The Healing Journey*. London: Darton Longman and Todd, 76.

7. Christianity

1 'Memories of a School Shooting: Paducah, Kentucky, 1997', *Atlantic*, 17 December 2012; www.theatlantic.com/national/archive/2012/12/memories-of-a-school-shooting-paducah-kentucky-1997/266358/.
2 Ruttenberg, Danya (2022), *On Repentance and Repair: Making Amends in an Unapologetic World*. Boston: Beacon Press, 187.
3 Sykes, Stephen (1977), *The Story of Atonement*. London: Darton Longman and Todd, 2.
4 As reported in *Time*, 1 June 1981, vol. 117, no. 22.
5 Biggar, Nigel, 'Melting the Icepacks of Enmity: Forgiveness and Reconciliation in Northern Ireland', *Studies in Christian Ethics* 24 (2), 201.
6 Levi, Primo (2000), *If This is a Man, The Truce*. London: Everyman's Library, 458.
7 'Opinion | The power of forgiveness in Charleston', *Washington Post*, 22 June 2015; www.washingtonpost.com/opinions/the-power-of-forgiveness/2015/06/22/a331c77e-190d-11e5-bd7f-4611a60dd8e5_story.html.
8 The interview can be heard here: 'Guatemala Nun', NPR, https://www.npr.org/1996/04/07/1008972/guatemala-nun
9 Keller, Timothy (2022), *Forgive: Why Should I and How Can I?* London: Hodder and Stoughton, 13.
10 Ruttenberg, op. cit., 171.
11 Ibid., 170.

8. Leadership

1 'Archbishop of Canterbury suggests Prince Andrew wants to "make amends"', Justin Welby, *Guardian*, 31 May 2022; www.theguardian.com/uk-news/2022/may/31/archbishop-of-canterbury-suggests-prince-andrew-wants-to-make-amends.

2 'We must learn how to forgive – and disagree', *Prospect Magazine*, 7 December 2018; www.prospectmagazine.co.uk/opinions/42016/justin-welby-we-must-learn-how-to-forgiveand-disagree.
3 Kendall, R. T. (2001), *Total Forgiveness: Achieving God's Greatest Challenge*. London: Hodder and Stoughton, 10.
4 Ibid., 176.
5 Hance, Stephen (2018), 'A Pastor Looks at Forgiveness', in Stephen Hance, ed., *Forgiveness in Practice*. London: Jessica Kingsley 128–136.
6 Ibid., 136.
7 Ibid.
8 Ibid., 134.
9 Wells, Samuel (2020), *Love Mercy: The Twelve Steps of Forgiveness*. London: Canterbury Press, x.
10 Ibid., 76.
11 Frances-Dehqani, Guli (2001), *Cries from a Lost Homeland: Reflections on Jesus' Sayings from the Cross*. London: Canterbury Press, 10.
12 Pastor Nadia Bolz-Weber, 'Forgive Assholes | Have a Little Faith,' YouTube.
13 quoted in Ruttenberg, op. cit., 179.
14 'Pardonne-Moi: On Vladimir Jankélévitch and the Philosophy of Forgiveness', *Los Angeles Review of Books*, 22 July 2021; lareviewofbooks.org/article/pardonne-moi-on-vladimir-jankelevitch-and-the-philosophy-of-forgiveness/.
15 Arendt, Hannah (2006), *Eichmann in Jerusalem: A Report on the Banality of Evil*. London: Penguin Classics, 278.

9. Karl

1 Wiesenthal, Simon (1998), *The Sunflower: On the Possibilities and Limits of Forgiveness*, revised edition. New York: Schocken Books.
2 Ibid., 43.
3 Ibid., 54.
4 Ibid., 55.
5 Ibid., 97–8.
6 Ibid., 55.

7 Ibid., 139.
8 Ibid., 268.
9 Ibid., 171.
10 Ibid., 136–7.
11 Ibid., 138.
12 Ibid., 182.
13 Ibid., 183.
14 Ibid., 132–2.
15 Ibid., 133.

10. Jesus

1 Potts, Matthew (2022), *Forgiveness – an Alternative Approach*. New Haven/London: Yale University Press, 5.
2 See Bash, Anthony, *Just Forgiveness: Exploring the Bible, Weighing the Issues* (London: SPCK, 2011) and *Forgiveness: A Theology* (Atlanta: Cascade, 2015).
3 Wells, op. cit., 80.
4 I explore the history of translation into English in more detail in my book on the Lord's Prayer, *Thy Will Be Done* (London, Bloomsbury, 2020), 118–22.
5 Church of England (2017), *Forgiveness and Reconciliation in the Aftermath of Abuse*. London: Church House Publishing, 88.
6 John Lippitt makes Wolterstorff's argument about care-*agape* a central role in his thinking about forgiveness as a 'work of love'. See Lippitt, John (2020), *Love's Forgiveness: Kierkegard, Resentment, Humility, and Hope*. Oxford: Oxford University Press, 114.
7 Cherry, Stephen (2016), *The Dark Side of the Soul: An Insider's Guide to the Web of Sin*. London: Bloomsbury.
8 John, Andy (2016), *Praying the Statues: A Lent Book*. Bangor: Bangor Diocesan Board of Finance, 39.

11. Repentance

1 Murphy, Jeffrie (2003), *Getting Even: Forgiveness and Its Limits*. Oxford: Oxford University Press, 77.
2 Zille, Tom (2020), 'A Change of Mind: The Reception of Treadwell Walden's *The Great Meaning of Metanoia* (1896)'. The University of Chicago Press.

3 'The beauty of change, of *metanoia*', *The Tablet*, 22 March 2022; www.thetablet.co.uk/texts-speeches-homilies/4/2027/the-beauty-of-change-of-metanoia#:~:-text=It%20does%2C%20of%20course%2C%20involve,God%20draws%20us%20to%20himself.
4 Konstan, David (2010), *Before Forgiveness: The Origins of a Moral Idea*. Cambridge: Cambridge University Press.

12. Repenting

1 Ruttenberg, op. cit.

13. Sorry

1 ''You have to let the anger go': Mina Smallman on her daughters' murder – and the police who shared photos of the bodies' *Guardian*, 26 May 2022; www.theguardian.com/world/2022/may/26/you-have-to-let-the-anger-go-mina-smallman-on-her-daughters-and-the-police-who-photographed-the-bodies.
2 Dorfman, Ariel (1996), *Death and the Maiden*. London: Nick Hern Books, 41.
3 Lapsley, Michael (2012), *Redeeming the Past: Journey from Freedom Fighter to Healer*. New York: Orbis Books, 151.
4 Fielding, Henry (1749), *Tom Jones*, Book 18, Chapter 12.
5 Little, Alistair with Ruth Scott (2009), *Give a Boy a Gun: From Killing to Peacemaking*. London: Darton, Longman and Todd, 192.
6 Cherry, Myisha, op. cit., 56.

14. Forgiving

1 'Gee Walker says, "I forgive them" to thugs who killed her son Anthony', *Liverpool Echo*, 30 November 2005; https://www.liverpoolecho.co.uk/news/tv/gee-walker-says-i-forgive-3525923.

15. Whirlpool

1 '"I forgive you": Charleston church victims' families confront suspect', *Guardian*, 20 June 2015; https://

www.theguardian.com/world/2015/jun/19/i-forgive-you-charleston-church-victims-families-confront-suspect.

2 Cherry writes, 'I use *racialized forgiveness* to refer to how race *negatively* influences whom we forgive; whose forgiveness we praise and criticize; *and* for what reason.' Cherry, Myisha (2021), 'Racialized Forgiveness' in *Hypatia* 36, 583–97.

3 Thurman, Howard (1976), *Jesus and the Disinherited*. Boston: Beacon Press, 69.

4 Ibid., 72.

5 Ibid., 76.

6 Ibid., 77.

7 Partington, Marian (2016), *If You Sit Very Still: A Sister's Fierce Engagement with Traumatic Loss*. London: Jessica Kingsley, 167–8.

17. Unforgivable?

1 The Anglican Consultative Council (at ACC-17) recommended guidelines for implementation by the provinces of the Anglican Communion (2019), *Anglican Communion Safe Church Commission* (www.anglicancommunion.org/media/349360/ACSCC-Guidelines-2019-English.pdf).

2 The Anglican Church Investigation Report: IICSA Independent Inquiry into Child Sexual Abuse, October 2020; https://www.iicsa.org.uk/reports-recommendations/publications/investigation/anglican-church.html.

3 Walker, Margaret Urban (2006), *Moral Repair: Reconstructing Moral Relations After Wrongdoing*. Cambridge: Cambridge University Press, 188. She is quoting an unpublished talk by Cheney Ryan, who said, 'Unforgivable acts are ones that *kill* hope.'